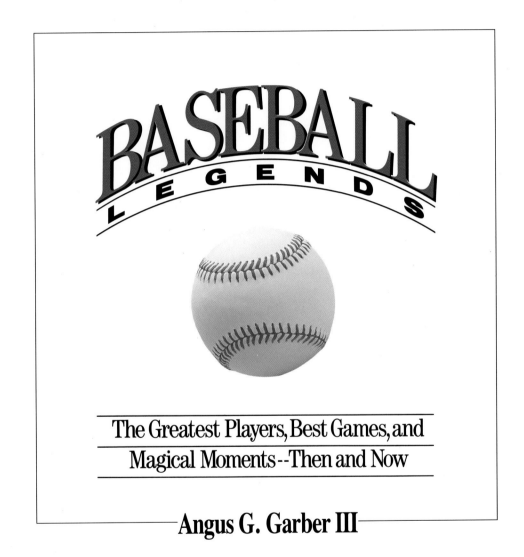

BASEBALL LEGENDS

The Greatest Players, Best Games, and
Magical Moments--Then and Now

Angus G. Garber III

GALLERY BOOKS
An Imprint of W.H. Smith Publishers Inc.
New York City 10016

A FRIEDMAN GROUP BOOK

Published by
GALLERY BOOKS
An imprint of W.H. Smith Publishers, Inc.
112 Madison Avenue
New York, New York 10016

ISBN 0-8317-0695-3

BASEBALL LEGENDS
was prepared and produced by
Michael Friedman Publishing Group, Inc.
15 West 26th Street
New York, New York 10010

Editor: Bruce Lubin
Art Director: Mary Moriarty
Designer: Rod Gonzalez
Photo Editor: Christine Cancelli
Production Manager: Karen L. Greenberg

Typeset by I, CLAVDIA Inc.
Color separations by South Sea Graphic Arts Company Ltd.
Printed and bound in Hong Kong by Leefung Asco Printers Ltd.

DEDICATION:

For my parents, Suzanne and Greg, who still labor under the impression that the Red Sox play football.

ACKNOWLEDGMENTS:

Thanks to those whose help made this book a reality: Claire Smith, the fine baseball writer for the Hartford Courant; Henry Gola, a terrific shortstop with a deep respect for the game; the fanatics at the Elias Sports Bureau; editor Bruce Lubin of the Michael Friedman Publishing Group; Mrs. Pat Kelly and Mr. Thomas Heitz, photo manager and librarian at Cooperstown; photo researcher Chris Cancelli; Joseph Reichler, whose *Baseball Encyclopedia* is probably the only place to discover that Pumpsi Green (.246 lifetime batting average) was born Elijah Jerry Green.

C O N T E N T S

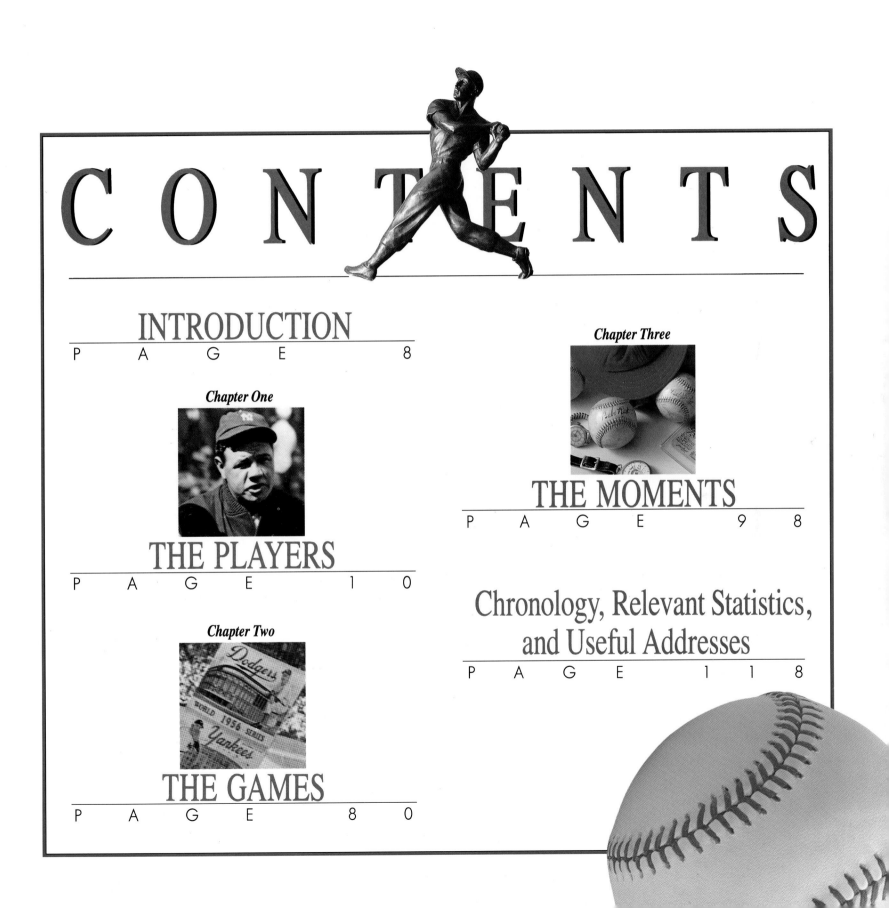

Introduction

Baseball enjoys a grip on nostalgia like no other sport. Although the world has changed over the last 100 years, baseball remains the same.

Baseball's timeless nature is no accident. When Alexander J. Cartwright organized the first game of baseball on June 19, 1846 in Hoboken, New Jersey, no clock was needed. And over the years, those who oversaw the evolution of the game left its beautiful symmetry untampered with. Today, baseball is the only major sport that doesn't limit itself within the framework of time, and perhaps that is one reason its appeal transcends all others.

A summer afternoon in the bleachers at Wrigley Field in Chicago can be a mystical experience. And later, on a crisp October night, the urgency of a World Series can suspend a city, if not an entire nation. Baseball is forever, of course, which is why little boys have been trading baseball cards since the turn of the century. The faces change but the game remains the same: vibrant and at once intellectual and visceral. It is why some little boys never grow up.

There are no penalties in baseball, save for taking a called third strike with two out in the bottom of the ninth. The fouls in baseball are not indiscretions committed with malice as in basketball or football, but merely unsuccessful attempts to place the ball in fair territory. Fair or foul. There isn't much of a gray area there. And might does not necessarily make right in this poetic game. No, baseball is fanfare for the common man of uncommon abilities. It isn't hard to relate to a 5-foot-9 shortstop who wears a cap, as opposed to a hulking 290-pound defensive tackle who grunts behind a menacing helmet.

Baseball endures. When Bill Veeck, the game's best salesman, suited up a midget wearing No. $\frac{1}{8}$ for the St. Louis Browns, in 1951, baseball, an institution that has always understood the difference between entertainment and dubious enterprise, didn't allow it to happen again. Controversial Oakland owner Charlie O.

An autographed baseball stays with a youngster forever. Even when he's seventy years old.

Finley tried to introduce day-glo orange baseballs and he, too, was given the thumb. One suspects that three strikes will always make an out.

And while labor disputes linger and salaries continue to spiral outrageously—the very best players make more than $2 million a year for playing a game—baseball is still one of the best places to escape this hopelessly complicated world. A day at the ballpark with a hot dog and an ice-cold beer will do that for you. Therapy never came cheaper.

Baseball's greatest gift is its unfailing flexibility. Nearly everything is defensible, in one way or another. To hit-and-run or play it safe? Do you let the number nine hitter swing away with a three-ball, one-strike count? Is a squeeze play advisable in this situation? Yes, and no, depending on who is making the decision and who is judging it with the benefit of hindsight.

Much of baseball's attraction is based on historical arguments. Was Honus Wagner, the Flying Dutchman who played from 1897 to 1917 and averaged .329, a better shortstop than Larry Bowa, the modern era player who led the National League in fielding percentage six times? Does Ty Cobb's best-ever .367 career batting average deserve an asterisk in the record book because he never played a 162-game schedule or a game under inadequate lights? Is Sandy Koufax, with 169 career victories, any less a pitcher than Gaylord Perry or Phil Niekro, who both achieved 300 wins in nearly twice as many games? Was Roger Maris' 61-home run season a better effort than Babe Ruth's 60-home run season, even though the Babe played in less games?

And thus the debates rage in barrooms and around kitchen tables, and probably always will. What follows are one fan's opinions.

The Bambino, second from the right, was the greatest legend of them all. He could pitch as well as hit. In fact, had he stuck with it, Babe Ruth might have reached Cooperstown as a pitcher.

The Players

The names come out of history, walking tall and swinging a big stick or throwing a fastball that explodes as it approaches home plate. They are baseball's most prized legends, happy possessions of an entire culture.

As of 1987, there were 199 players enshrined in the National Baseball Hall of Fame at Cooperstown, New York. Many of the names roll easily off the tongue of even the casual baseball fan: Ruth, Aaron, Mays, Gehrig. They also include players like Jake Beckley, the first baseman who knocked in 1,574 runs from 1888 to 1907. And Mordecai "Three Fingers" Brown, the right-hander for St. Louis, Chicago, and Cincinnati with 239 career victories and an earned run average of 2.06. Also enshrined is Elmer Flick, a 5-foot-9 right fielder at the turn of the century who batted .315 for a career of 13 years.

What separates the Ruths from the Flicks? In some cases, not a lot. Assembled here is a roster of baseball's truly great players. They are included not merely on the basis of their weighty statistics, but their total contributions to the game. For instance, Brooks Robinson's .267 career batting average is one of the Hall of Fame's lowest, but his deft glove at third base made defense fashionable again.

Hank Aaron hit 755 home runs, the all-time record, and Pete Rose hit more than 3,000 singles, which helped him break Ty Cobb's record of 4,191 hits. Cy Young won 511 games, or exactly 346 more than Sandy Koufax. All are undeniably the stuff of legends.

HANK AARON

Although he hit only 13 homers his first full season in the Big Leagues, Hank Aaron averaged 34 home runs for each of the next 22 seasons.

Aaron's major league record of 6,856 total bases is 722 more than Stan Musial's second-place total.

He is the first name in *The Baseball Encyclopedia* and the last name in home runs. He is, of course, Hank Louis Aaron, who leads the way alphabetically and by glorious example.

Aaron, economical and brilliantly consistent, endured for 24 years and broke many important slugging records. The 6-foot, 185-pound Mobile, Alabama right-hander passed Babe Ruth's cherished milestone of 714 home runs on April 4, 1974 and didn't stop until he reached 755, as imposing a number as there is in baseball. There are others: 2,297 runs batted in, 6,856 total bases, 1,477 extra-base hits—major-league records all.

Hammerin' Hank made 24 All-Star game appearances and compiled a marvelous .305 batting average. His muscular line drives led to two National League batting titles, something unusual for a player of such strength.

Aaron had left home at the age of seventeen with two dollars in his pocket, two sandwiches in his hand and two pairs of pants. His first train ride took him to the Indianapolis Clowns, a barnstorming team. The following year he became the shortstop for Eau Claire in the Northern League and batted .336, but hit only nine home runs. After a season at Jacksonville of the South Atlantic League (22 home runs), Aaron was ready to join the Milwaukee Braves. He was thrown into an uncertain outfield situation and came up swinging. The home runs (13) weren't there quite yet, but a .280 batting average and respectable runs batted in (69) and runs scored (58) offered a promising future.

No one was prepared for what followed. It wasn't that Aaron exploded on the scene, drawing the eyes of the baseball world; Willie Mays and Mickey Mantle were still the leading lights of the major leagues. No, Aaron started putting together one muscular season after another. First came his impressive 1957 effort: 44 home runs, 132 runs batted in, 118 runs scored, and a batting average of .322. Then, in 1963, Aaron produced nearly identical numbers: 44 home runs, 130 runs batted in, 121 runs scored, and a .319 average. Such was his greatest gift: To reproduce that magnificent swing again and again.

Aaron never enjoyed a 50-home run season the way Ruth, Maris, Mantle, and Mays did, but he averaged 33 homers a year, and exactly 100 runs batted in. Only Ty Cobb produced more runs than Hank Aaron's 3,716.

When it was all over, Aaron had done it all. In 1957, he had won the league's Most Valuable Player award and hit three home runs as the Braves won the World Series. And because he is first in home runs by such a wide margin, Aaron's record is sure to last.

It's a round ball and a round bat and you've got to hit it square. No one was squarer than Henry Aaron.

S T A T S

YEAR	G	AB	H	2B	3B	HR	TB	R	RBI	BB	AVG
1954	122	468	131	27	6	13	209	58	69	28	.280
1955	153	602	189	37	9	27	325	105	106	49	.314
1956	153	609	200	34	14	26	340	106	92	37	.328
1957	151	615	198	27	6	44	369	118	132	57	.322
1958	153	601	196	34	4	30	328	109	95	59	.326
1959	154	629	223	46	7	39	400	116	123	51	.355
1960	153	590	172	20	11	40	334	102	126	60	.292
1961	155	603	197	39	10	34	358	115	120	56	.327
1962	156	592	191	28	6	45	366	127	128	66	.323
1963	161	631	201	29	4	44	370	121	130	78	.319
1964	145	570	187	30	2	24	293	103	95	62	.328
1965	150	570	181	40	1	32	319	109	89	60	.318
1966	158	603	168	23	1	44	325	117	127	76	.279
1967	155	600	184	37	3	39	344	113	109	63	.307
1968	160	606	174	33	4	29	302	84	86	64	.287
1969	147	547	164	30	3	44	332	100	97	87	.300
1970	150	516	154	26	1	38	296	103	118	74	.298
1971	139	495	162	22	3	47	331	95	118	71	.327
1972	129	449	119	10	0	34	231	75	77	92	.265
1973	120	392	118	12	1	40	252	84	96	68	.301
1974	112	340	91	16	0	20	167	47	69	39	.268
1975	137	465	109	16	2	12	165	45	60	70	.234
1976	85	271	62	8	0	10	100	22	35	35	.229
TOTAL	**3298**	**12364**	**3771**	**624**	**98**	**755**	**6856**	**2174**	**2297**	**1402**	**.305**

Although he played in 14 pennant-winning Yankee seasons, Yogi Berra came home to the other New York team—the Mets—in 1972. The next year, they were in the World Series.

YOGI BERRA

Berra uttered the unforgettable quote: "It ain't over 'til it's over."

Of course, many people believe that the contributions of Lawrence Peter Berra are confined solely to his creative assaults on the English language. Well, it just ain't so.

Yogi Berra was a pretty fair ballplayer in his day. He wasn't the fastest runner on the bases, but what would you expect from a 5-foot-7, 185-pound catcher? True, his career batting average was a modest .285. And, certainly, the left-hander never hit more than 30 home runs in a season. He never led the American League in any meaningful offensive statistic. All he did was win.

Berra played on 14 New York Yankees pennant-winning teams and was a member of 10 world championship outfits. He was a three-time league Most Valuable Player and was selected to 15 consecutive All-Star games. Certainly, he played in the gifted company of pinstripers like Joe DiMaggio, Phil Rizzuto, Whitey Ford, Billy Martin, Mickey Mantle, and Roger Maris, but Berra set the standard for winning. No one may ever equal his consistent success.

Bucky Harris discovered him in Newark, New Jersey. Harris, then the skipper in Buffalo, saw the St. Louis-born Berra and raved about him to the New York brass. When he took over as New York's manager in 1947, Harris made Berra his special project, and helped make him into a major league hitter. It required a lot of patience. On one occasion, Berra—a compulsive swinger in his early days—took three straight strikes and walked back to the dugout with obvious disgust. "It's all your fault, Bucky," Berra said. "How do you expect a guy to hit and think at the same time?"

In time, Berra learned. In 1950 he had his best season, with a .322 batting average, 28 home runs, 124 runs batted in, and 116 runs scored. From 1953 to 1956, he drove in 100 runs every season. Meanwhile, Berra had learned the craft of catching from Hall of Famer Bill Dickey and Yogi handled the Yankees' talented staff beautifully.

In 75 World Series games, Berra hit 12 home runs, scored 41 runs and knocked in 39.

After a 19-year career, Berra went on to manage the Yankees and Mets to pennants in 1964 and 1973, respectively. He just couldn't stop winning. With Yogi Berra, it was never over until his team had won.

S T A T S

YEAR	G	AB	H	2B	3B	HR	TB	R	RBI	BB	AVG
1946	7	22	8	1	0	2	15	3	4	1	.364
1947	83	293	82	15	3	11	136	41	54	13	.280
1948	125	469	143	24	10	14	229	70	98	25	.305
1949	116	415	115	20	2	20	199	59	91	22	.277
1950	151	597	192	30	6	28	318	116	124	55	.322
1951	141	547	161	19	4	27	269	92	88	44	.294
1952	142	534	146	17	1	30	255	97	98	66	.273
1953	137	503	149	23	5	27	263	80	108	50	.296
1954	151	584	179	28	6	22	285	88	125	56	.307
1955	147	541	147	20	3	27	254	84	108	60	.272
1956	140	521	155	29	2	30	278	93	105	65	.298
1957	134	482	121	14	2	24	211	74	82	57	.251
1958	122	433	115	17	3	22	204	60	90	35	.266
1959	131	472	134	25	1	19	218	64	69	43	.284
1960	120	359	99	14	1	15	160	46	62	38	.276
1961	119	395	107	11	0	22	184	62	61	35	.271
1962	86	232	52	8	0	10	90	25	35	24	.224
1963	64	147	43	6	0	8	73	20	28	15	.293
1965	4	9	2	0	0	0	2	1	0	0	.222
TOTAL	2120	7555	2150	321	49	358	3643	1175	1430	704	.285

BASEBALL
LEGENDS
The Players

STEVE CARLTON

From 1967 through 1984, Carlton won 13 games or more in 17 of 18 seasons.

They called him "Lefty" and in many ways he was the prototypical left-handed pitcher.

Stephen Norman Carlton did not have a blinding fastball, though it sailed past most batters in Carlton's prime. His out pitch was a slider, supported by a nasty curveball. Only one man in the history of baseball (Nolan Ryan) made batters miss more often. Through 1986, the 6-foot-4, 210-pound Carlton had amassed the staggering total of 4,044 strikeouts. Walter Johnson, Tom Seaver, Bob Gibson, and Cy Young all fell well short of that mark. Carlton's victory total of 323 placed him among the very best totals.

Carlton endured. For 18 consecutive seasons he won in double figures; five times, he won 20 games in a season. He won the National League's Cy Young Award three times in a way no one else has. In 1972, his first season after leaving the St. Louis Cardinals, Carlton gave the Philadelphia Phillies the best year of his career, winning 27 games. He struck out 310 batters that year, posted an earned run average of 1.97, and completed 30 games—all figures that led the National League. Then, five seasons later, Carlton won the Cy Young again. The numbers in 1977: a 23-10 record, a 2.64 earned run average, 198 strikeouts. Five more seasons passed before Carlton claimed the Cy Young for a third time, tying the league record of Sandy Koufax and Tom Seaver. That year Carlton, then 37, went 23-11, with 286 strikeouts and six shutouts. While Koufax won his three Cy Youngs in a span of four years and Seaver required six years, Carlton's excellence spanned 11 years. The next year, Carlton came back and won the league's strikeout title, fanning an improbable 275 batters.

For years, Carlton has suffered in the shadow of Ryan. The year Carlton struck out a career-high 310, Ryan registered 329 strikeouts. Ryan will finish his career as baseball's top strikeout artist and Carlton is destined for second place. Yet what many fail to remember is that Ryan consistently has been a .500 pitcher over his career, while Carlton had won 100 more games than he lost.

History, at least, will judge Carlton as one of the best.

S T A T S

YEAR	G	W	L	IP	SO	TBB	GS	CG	ShO	ERA
1965	15	0	0	25	21	8	2	0	0	2.52
1966	9	3	3	52	25	18	9	2	1	3.12
1967	30	14	9	193	168	62	28	11	2	2.98
1968	34	13	11	232	162	61	33	10	5	2.99
1969	31	17	11	236	210	93	31	12	2	2.17
1970	34	10	19	254	193	109	33	13	2	3.72
1971	37	20	9	273	172	98	36	18	4	3.56
1972	41	27	10	346	310	87	41	30	8	1.97
1973	40	13	20	293	223	113	40	18	3	3.90
1974	39	16	13	291	240	136	39	17	1	3.22
1975	37	15	14	255	192	104	37	14	3	3.56
1976	35	20	7	253	195	72	35	13	2	3.13
1977	36	23	10	283	198	89	36	17	2	2.64
1978	34	16	13	247	161	63	34	12	3	2.84
1979	35	18	11	251	213	89	35	13	4	3.62
1980	38	24	9	304	286	90	38	13	3	2.34
1981	24	13	4	190	179	62	24	10	1	2.42
1982	38	23	11	296	286	86	38	19	6	3.10
1983	37	15	16	284	275	84	37	8	3	3.12
1984	33	13	7	229	163	79	33	1	0	3.58
1985	16	1	8	92	48	53	16	0	0	3.33
1986	32	9	14	177	120	86	32	0	0	3.69
TOTAL	**705**	**323**	**229**	**5056**	**4040**	**1742**	**687**	**251**	**55**	**3.11**

Steve Carlton was one of baseball's most durable pitchers. In his later years, he mastered the martial arts to keep his slider fresh.

TY COBB

Although Cobb is known primarily as a hitter, he stole home plate 35 times—by far the most ever by a major leaguer.

He was the definition of hubris, but Tyrus Raymond Cobb never failed to deliver on a challenge. As Pete Rose, himself a notoriously fierce competitor, said as he closed in on Cobb's all-time record for hits, "I think I would have liked the guy."

No doubt. Clearly Ty Cobb stands as one of the game's greatest players ever; his 6-foot-1, 175-pound frame was at least three-quarters heart. The rest was spit and vinegar. Even his teammates hated him. Detroit manager Hughey Jennings had two sets of rules—one for the Tigers and the other for Cobb, who broke in 1905. "When you play like him," Jennings said, "you'll get special treatment too."

Cobb was only an average center fielder, but he knew how to play the hitters. His terrific speed neutralized any errors in outfield judgment. Hitting was something else, however. Though he hit only .240 as a rookie, Cobb batted .350 in 1907 and carried Detroit to its first of three consecutive American League pennants. It was the first of 23 straight seasons over .300, including 12 batting titles, nine of them in a row—his first at the age of twenty.

Cobb's career batting average of .367 may never be equalled. After Rogers Hornsby (.358) and Dan Brouthers (.349) no one is even close. Three times, he hit .400, most notably in 1911, when he compiled 248 hits for a .420 average. That was the year Cobb scored 147 runs, knocked in another 144, hit 47 doubles, 24 triples, stole 83 bases, and slugged .621, league-leading totals all. And most of Cobb's 4,191 hits came in the days of the dead ball, when umpires left baseballs in play until the seams were loose. Only Rose finished his career with more hits.

Cobb's consistency was startling. In 1927, at age 41, he hit .357 for the Philadelphia Athletics, stole 22 bases and drove in 93 runs. And as devastating as Cobb was from the left side of home plate, it was the pure arrogance of his base-running ability that left opponents shattered.

There were times when he would intentionally force the issue, knowing the other team was more likely to make a mistake than he. Cobb stole 892 bases during his career, 96 of them swiped in 1915. That record lasted until Maury Wills stole 104 in 1962. The sight of Cobb's shining spikes left many infielders worrying more about their well-being than tagging him out. He once spiked the Giants' Charlie Herzog in an exhibition game. Thus was his competitive nature.

It was this competitive drive which consumed him. "I got to be first—all the time," Cobb once told a teammate. Most of the time, he was.

The cloud of dust tells the story: Ty Cobb could never stand still—not when there was a base to be stolen.

BASEBALL
LEGENDS
The Players

*Note the intent gaze, the concentration.
It carried Ty Cobb to a lifetime batting
average of .367.*

S T A T S

YEAR	G	AB	H	2B	3B	HR	TB	R	RBI	BB	AVG
1905	41	150	36	6	0	1	45	19	15	10	.240
1906	98	358	113	13	7	1	143	45	41	19	.316
1907	150	605	212	29	15	5	286	97	116	24	.350
1908	150	581	188	36	20	4	276	88	101	34	.324
1909	156	573	216	33	10	9	296	116	115	48	.377
1910	140	508	194	35	13	8	279	106	88	64	.382
1911	146	591	248	47	24	8	367	147	144	44	.420
1912	140	553	227	30	23	7	324	119	90	43	.410
1913	122	428	167	18	16	4	229	70	67	58	.390
1914	97	345	127	22	11	2	177	69	57	57	.368
1915	156	563	208	31	13	3	274	144	99	118	.369
1916	145	542	201	31	10	5	267	113	68	78	.371
1917	152	588	225	44	23	7	336	107	102	61	.383
1918	111	421	161	19	14	3	217	83	64	41	.382
1919	124	497	191	36	13	1	256	92	70	38	.384
1920	112	428	143	28	8	2	193	86	63	58	.334
1921	128	507	197	37	16	12	302	124	101	56	.389
1922	137	526	211	42	16	4	297	99	99	55	.401
1923	145	556	189	40	7	6	261	103	88	66	.340
1924	155	625	211	38	10	4	281	115	74	85	.338
1925	121	415	157	31	12	12	248	97	102	65	.378
1926	79	233	79	18	5	4	119	48	62	26	.339
1927	133	490	175	32	7	5	236	104	93	67	.357
1928	95	353	114	27	4	1	152	54	40	34	.323
TOTAL	3033	11436	4190	723	297	118	5861	2245	1959	1249	.367

JOE DiMAGGIO

In DiMaggio's hands, the bat became almost a living thing. At times it looked like an extension of his arm.

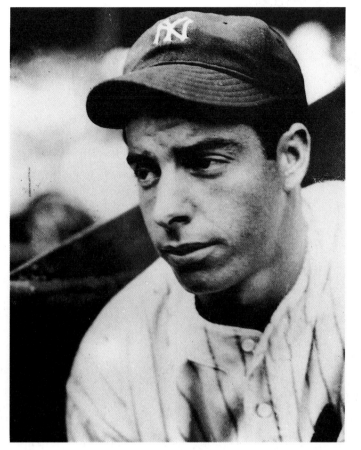

In only his second season (1937) DiMaggio hit 46 home runs to lead the major leagues.

Surely, Joe DiMaggio was *the* baseball player's player. He was almost ethereal gliding around in center field at Yankee Stadium, and his graceful swing and follow-through appeared unconsciously efficient, like the man himself. "The Yankee Clipper," or "Joltin' Joe," if you prefer, was 6-foot-2, 193 pounds of smooth. It was all so easy. Too easy, some thought.

Forget the innate hitting ability for a moment. DiMaggio's teammates swear they never saw him make a mental error in thirteen years of playing for the Yankees. Thirteen years without a mistake in judgment? Well, once he attempted to stretch a single into a double and was called out against the Red Sox. The umpire, reportedly, admitted later that he had missed the call.

A skinny kid with a wide stance, he was discovered by Yankees' scout Bill Essick, who recommended in 1934 that General Manager Ed Barrow buy him from the San Francisco Seals. It cost New York only $25,000, five minor league players and an agreement to wait one season. DiMaggio, who finished the 1934 season with a .341 batting average, led the Seals to the Pacific Coast League title in 1935 with a .398 average, 34 home runs and 154 runs batted in. He was viewed as something of a savior when he arrived in New York. After all, the Yankees had won only one pennant in seven years.

DiMaggio delivered with a .323 average, 29 home runs, and 125 runs batted in, helping New York win the World Series for the first time since 1932. They played in the Fall Classic six times in DiMaggio's first seven seasons. He was a two-time batting champion, hitting .381 and .352 in 1939 and 1940. DiMaggio was named Most Valuable Player of the American League three times. His 361 career homers and 1,537 runs batted in were remarkable numbers for a player who lost three seasons to the war effort.

The thing people remember most, however, is DiMaggio's 56-game hitting streak, authored in 1941. It is recognized today as baseball's most difficult feat of all time. It is a record that may never be broken and is a testament to DiMaggio's remarkable talents, ability to persevere, and his unearthly powers of concentration. With Joe DiMaggio at the plate, though, it looked *so* easy.

Joe DiMaggio was a thin man, but
somewhere he found the power to hit
361 career home runs. Timing, he said,
was everything.

							S	T	A	T	S				
YEAR	G	AB	H	2B	3B	HR	TB	R	RBI	BB	AVG
1936	138	637	206	44	15	29	367	132	125	24	.323
1937	151	621	215	35	15	46	418	151	167	64	.346
1938	145	599	194	32	13	32	348	129	140	59	.324
1939	120	462	176	32	6	30	310	108	126	52	.381
1940	132	508	179	28	9	31	318	93	133	61	.352
1941	139	541	193	43	11	30	348	122	125	76	.357
1942	154	610	186	29	13	21	304	123	114	68	.305
1946	132	503	146	20	8	25	257	81	95	59	.290
1947	141	534	168	31	10	20	279	97	97	64	.315
1948	153	594	190	26	11	39	355	110	155	67	.320
1949	76	272	94	14	6	14	162	58	67	55	.346
1950	139	525	158	33	10	32	307	114	122	80	.301
1951	116	415	109	22	4	12	175	72	71	61	.263
TOTAL	1736	6821	2214	389	131	361	3948	1390	1537	790	.325

LOU GEHRIG

Gehrig hit 23 career grand slams, the major-league record. Babe Ruth managed only 16.

When Wally Pipp wasn't up to playing first base for the New York Yankees one day in 1925, Lou Gehrig stepped into the lineup. He didn't come out for 2,130 games. Let there be no doubt why Gehrig was known as "The Iron Man." And yet, there are many more reasons why he is considered the greatest first baseman ever.

He broke the consecutive-game record of 1,307 set by L. Everett Scott, the shortstop for Boston and New York from 1914 to 1926. Gehrig's monstrous achievement remains a record today, and an unassailable one at that. Steve Garvey, playing for the Los Angeles Dodgers in the 1970s, put together a highly publicized run of 1,207 straight games for the third-best total ever. Garvey would have needed nearly six more seasons without a miss to pass Gehrig. But as breathtaking as that record of durability is, Gehrig's greatest contributions to the Yankees came from his bat.

Henry Louis Gehrig was born in New York, attended Columbia University, and in 1923, at the age of 20, found himself playing for the Yankees. Along with Babe Ruth, Gehrig formed baseball's most formidable and celebrated one-two punch. In 1927, Ruth, Gehrig, Bob Meusel, and Tony Lazzeri formed the middle of the lineup known as "Murderers' Row." That Yankees team won 100 games and swept Pittsburgh 4-0 in the World Series.

There may never have been a better team, and Gehrig was at the heart of it. In the American League that year, Ruth hit his magnificent 60 home runs, but Gehrig came in an impressive second with 47. Lazzeri's 18 were good for third, which says something about Ruth and Gehrig's dominance. Gehrig edged Ruth in the RBI department, 175-164, and in total bases, 447-417. Ruth and Gehrig were also one-two in runs scored, slugging percentage, and walks.

Gehrig hit .373 that year and averaged .340 for his 17-year career. His consistent power echoed his ability to play every day. For 13 straight seasons, Gehrig drove in more than 100 runs. He led the league five times in that category and finished his career with 1,991, a figure only Ruth and Hank Aaron surpassed. Three of the best six season RBI totals belong to Gehrig. And he scored 1,888 runs, a total that also ranks among the very best efforts of all-time.

He was always on the leading edge. In 1932, Gehrig became the first 20th century player to hit four consecutive home runs in one game. His World Series performances were superb: in 34 games, Gehrig hit 10 home runs, knocked in 35 runs, scored 30, and batted .361. It doesn't get much better than that. Durable numbers, to be sure.

Back in his Ivy League days at Columbia, no one could have predicted that Lou Gehrig would have become such a phenomenal superstar.

S T A T S

YEAR	G	AB	H	2B	3B	HR	TB	R	RBI	BB	AVG
1923	13	26	11	4	1	1	20	6	9	2	.423
1924	10	12	6	1	0	0	7	2	6	1	.500
1925	126	437	129	23	10	20	232	73	68	46	.295
1926	155	572	179	47	20	16	314	135	107	105	.313
1927	155	584	218	52	18	47	447	149	175	109	.373
1928	154	562	210	47	13	27	364	139	142	95	.374
1929	154	553	166	33	9	35	322	127	126	122	.300
1930	154	581	220	42	17	41	419	143	174	101	.379
1931	155	619	211	31	15	46	410	163	184	117	.341
1932	156	596	208	42	9	34	370	138	151	108	.349
1933	152	593	198	41	12	32	359	138	139	92	.334
1934	154	579	210	40	6	49	409	128	165	109	.363
1935	149	535	176	26	10	30	312	125	119	132	.329
1936	155	579	205	37	7	49	403	167	152	130	.354
1937	157	569	200	37	9	37	366	138	159	127	.351
1938	157	576	170	32	6	29	301	115	114	107	.295
1939	8	28	4	0	0	0	4	2	1	5	.143
TOTAL	2164	8001	2721	535	162	493	5059	1888	1991	1508	.340

Lou Gehrig was baseball's "Iron Man."
For 2,130 games he never took a break.

BOB GIBSON

Fueled by the fire within, Bob Gibson was one of the most tenacious pitchers in baseball. He was also one of the best.

Gibson set a record by winning seven straight World Series games for the Cardinals from 1964 to 1968.

Robert "Hoot" Gibson nicely summed up his wonderful pitching life in his autobiography, *From Ghetto to Glory.* That's how it happened.

Born in 1935 in a four-room Omaha, Nebraska shack, Gibson learned at an early age to make the most of his opportunities, and for 17 years the 6-foot-1, 189-pound right-hander capitalized on behalf of the St. Louis Cardinals. In an eight-year period, Gibson averaged nearly 20 victories a season as the Cardinals' stopper.

His first five seasons in the majors passed uneventfully. Though Gibson carried a 34-36 record into the 1963 season, there were signs he could pitch. Although he led the National League with 119 walks in 1961, he also managed to strike out 166. The next year there were five shutouts, a league-leading total. Gibson honed his fastball and slider and his control improved; he was to strike out 200 batters or more for nine of the next 11 seasons.

In the big games, Gibson loomed larger than life. In his first World Series, in 1964, Gibson struck out 31 New York Yankees and won his last two decisions with complete games. In 1967, he personally beat the Boston Red Sox, winning all three of his starts and throwing a three-hitter in the deciding seventh game. Overall, Gibson finished with an earned run average of 1.00. He struck out 26 batters and walked only 5.

And then in 1968, Gibson entered another dimension. He won 22 games and lost only nine. The stunning earned run average of 1.12 is the fourth-best effort in history. He threw 268 strikeouts, compared to 62 bases on balls. At one point in the torrid season, Gibson won 15 straight games.

In the World Series opener on October 2, Gibson fanned 17 Detroit Tigers, a World Series record. He won a 4-0 shutout and came back with a 10-strikeout performance in the fourth game, a 10-1 romp. In losing the seventh game, 4-1, Gibson struck out eight more batters to set a single World Series record of 35 strikeouts. Gibson, understandably, was the National League's Most Valuable Player that year and the Cy Young Award winner.

In 1970, Gibson won the Cy Young again with a record of 23-7 and 274 strikeouts. The next year, at age 35, he no-hit the Pittsburgh Pirates. He led the league in shutouts that season with 5, covering himself with glory again. With mental and athletic ferocity, Gibson dominated the competition.

S T A T S

YEAR	G	W	L	IP	SO	TBB	GS	CG	ShO	ERA
1959	13	3	5	76	48	39	9	2	1	3.33
1960	27	3	6	87	69	48	12	2	0	5.61
1961	35	13	12	211	166	119	27	10	2	3.24
1962	32	15	13	234	208	95	30	15	5	2.85
1963	36	18	9	255	204	96	33	14	2	3.39
1964	40	19	12	287	245	86	36	17	2	3.01
1965	38	20	12	299	270	103	36	30	6	3.07
1966	35	21	12	280	225	78	35	20	5	2.44
1967	24	13	7	175	147	40	24	10	2	2.98
1968	34	22	9	305	268	62	24	28	13	1.12
1969	35	20	13	314	269	95	35	28	4	2.18
1970	34	23	7	294	274	88	34	23	3	3.12
1971	31	16	13	246	185	76	31	20	5	3.04
1972	34	19	11	278	208	88	34	23	4	2.46
1973	25	12	10	195	142	57	25	13	1	2.77
1974	33	11	13	240	129	104	33	9	1	3.83
1975	22	3	10	109	60	62	14	1	0	5.04
TOTAL	**528**	**251**	**174**	**3885**	**3117**	**1336**	**472**	**265**	**56**	**2.91**

REGGIE JACKSON

Reggie. He was a single-name enterprise who was truly global in scope. Just ask him.

Through 1986, Jackson had established a major league record with 2,500 strikeouts.

Even when he missed, which was often enough, Reginald Martinez Jackson was exciting. His helmet would fly off and he would twist off balance in the batter's box. No matter, he had two more strikes. And it was Jackson's singular charisma that kept you in your seat wondering whether he was going to put one out or go down swinging—rarely looking.

Every goal has its price and strikeouts (some 2,500) were a small piece of change considering the 548 home runs Jackson had produced—created might be a better word—through 1986. That placed him sixth on the all-time list, ahead of people like Mantle, Foxx, Williams, and Gehrig.

Jackson was born in Wyncote, Pennsylvania and first rose to prominence at Arizona State University. The 6-foot, 206-pound outfielder was drafted second overall by the Kansas City Athletics in the 1966 free agent draft and one year later he was playing with the big club. The A's moved to Oakland in 1968 and Jackson's first full year in the major leagues was notable for 29 home runs and also 171 strikeouts, a league-leading figure. That success/failure ratio would hold up for most of his career.

Reggie—how many people in this world can be identified by a single name?—called himself "the straw that stirs the drink" and he in turn stirred the hearts of many for the better part of two decades. "Mr. October" performed best under the bright lights and cameras of post-season play. Indeed, his World Series record is unimpeachable.

Jackson hit .310 in his first two World Series when the A's defeated the New York Mets and Los Angeles Dodgers in 1973 and 1974. Facing elimination in the sixth game against the Mets, the A's turned to Jackson. He knocked in Oakland's first two runs with doubles in the first and third innings, then singled and scored the third in a 3-1 victory. In the seventh game, Jackson and Bert Campaneris hit two-run home runs in the third inning of a game the A's would win 5-2.

In 1977 Jackson offered one of the most memorable World Series performances in history. He had moved from Oakland to Baltimore in 1976 and again to the Yankees a year later. Heading into game six with a 3-2 lead in the series, New York was looking to finish off the Los Angeles Dodgers. Jackson, who had already homered twice in the Series, walked on four pitches from Burt Hooten the first time up. In the bottom of the fourth, Jackson took Hooten's first pitch over the right field fence for a two-run homer. That gave the Yankees a 4-3 lead. His next time at bat Jackson deposited Elias Sosa's first pitch even farther back than his first home run, and the score was 7-3. Two swings, two home runs. And as Jackson came to the plate in the eighth inning, the New York fans were on their feet. Jackson stepped in against knuckleballer Charlie Hough, an unlikely home run victim, but sure enough, the first pitch landed 450 feet away in the center-field bleachers. Jackson stopped to drink it all in and 90 feet down the first baseline Dodgers first baseman Steve Garvey was applauding in his glove. Three swings, three home runs. History. Reggie.

BASEBALL
LEGENDS
The Players

In 1967, Reggie came to bat for the Kansas City Athletics. Two decades later, his stance remains the same.

YEAR	G	AB	H	2B	3B	HR	TB	R	RBI	BB	AVG
1967	35	118	21	4	4	1	36	13	6	10	.178
1968	154	553	138	13	6	29	250	82	74	50	.250
1969	152	549	151	36	3	47	334	123	118	114	.275
1970	149	426	101	21	2	23	195	57	66	75	.237
1971	150	567	157	29	3	32	288	87	80	63	.277
1972	135	499	132	25	2	25	236	72	75	59	.265
1973	151	539	158	28	2	32	286	99	117	76	.293
1974	148	506	146	25	1	29	260	90	93	86	.289
1975	157	593	150	39	3	36	303	91	104	67	.253
1976	134	498	138	27	2	27	250	84	91	54	.277
1977	146	525	150	39	2	32	289	93	110	75	.286
1978	139	511	140	13	5	27	244	82	97	58	.274
1979	131	465	138	24	2	29	253	78	89	65	.297
1980	143	514	154	22	4	41	307	94	111	83	.300
1981	94	334	79	17	1	15	143	33	54	46	.237
1982	153	530	146	17	1	39	282	92	101	85	.275
1983	116	397	77	14	1	14	135	43	49	52	.194
1984	143	525	117	17	2	25	213	67	81	55	.223
1985	143	460	116	27	0	27	224	64	85	78	.252
1986	132	419	101	12	2	18	171	65	58	92	.241
TOTAL	2705	9528	2510	449	48	548	4699	1509	1659	1343	.263

S T A T S

Star quality is bringing the fans out of
their seats on a swing and a miss.

WALTER JOHNSON

Johnson's 113 career shutouts are an all-time major league high; 38 of them were 1-0 complete games.

Twenty victories in a season is the recognized standard of excellence for a pitcher. Most go an entire career failing to reach that milestone, while some of the better craftsmen manage the feat once or twice. Walter Perry "The Big Train" Johnson did it 12 times—for a losing team, the Washington Senators.

He went straight to the majors out of Humboldt, Kansas, a right-handed fireballer of 19. In 1910, his fourth season, Johnson won 25 games and lost 17. It was the beginning of a decade in which every season brought with it a 20-game season by Johnson. During that time, he won 264 games and lost 143. Those victories represented more than a third of the games the Senators managed to win during that time.

Johnson, at 6-foot-1, 200 pounds, was an imposing figure on the mound, though warm and affable off it. When he dropped to a three-quarters or sidearm motion he was pretty near impossible to hit. They didn't have radar guns in those days, but Johnson most certainly was in a class with Nolan Ryan, whose fastball has been clocked at over 100 miles an hour. And Johnson could put it anywhere he wanted.

Although Johnson developed a curveball that he was quite proud of, it was his fastball that left them swinging at air. Johnson struck out 3,506 batters, a record that stood for 54 years until Gaylord Perry broke it in 1983. In 1910, Johnson struck out 313 batters in 374 innings. He fanned 303 two years later while winning 32 games. In 1913, Johnson had the greatest year ever by a pitcher, going 36-7 with an earned run average of 1.14. He led the American League with 30 complete games, 12 shutouts, 243 strikeouts—and less than one walk per nine innings.

The list of accomplishments is staggering. Only Cy Young had more than Johnson's lifetime 416 victories. He once pitched 56 consecutive scoreless innings and in 1912 Johnson won 16 games in a row, something anyone has yet to surpass. And this was for a team that was generally awful. There was one, brief shining season, though.

In 1924, at age 37, Johnson pitched the Senators to the American League pennant. He was 23-7, though he had lost a yard on his fastball. He hadn't won 20 games for four seasons, but with Goose Goslin hitting .344 and knocking in 129 runs, Washington reached the World Series. Johnson lost his first two decisions to the New York Giants and came back with a masterful seventh-game effort. He pitched 12 innings, allowing only three runs, and was on base when Earl McNeely's grounder to third hit a pebble and took a wild hop over the head of Giants third baseman Fred Lindstrom. Muddy Ruel flew home with the winning run. It was Washington's first and only world championship.

A familiar story underlines Johnson's marvelous talent. Cleveland shortstop Ray Chapman once watched two fastballs sail past him at the plate, threw his bat down and headed for the dugout. "That's only strike two," hollered umpire Billy Evans.

"I know," Chapman said. "You can have the next one, it won't do me any good."

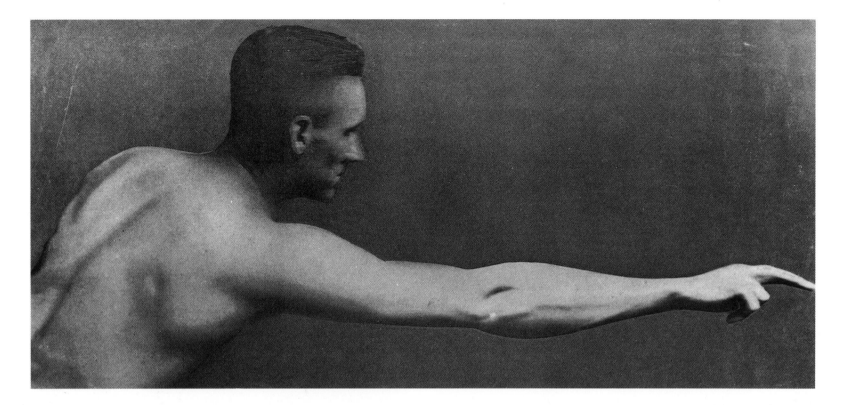

S T A T S

YEAR	G	W	L	IP	SO	TBB	GS	CG	ShO	ERA
1907	14	5	9	111	70	17	12	11	2	1.87
1908	36	14	14	257	160	53	29	23	6	1.64
1909	40	13	25	297	164	84	36	27	4	2.21
1910	45	25	17	373	313	76	42	38	8	1.35
1911	40	25	13	323	207	70	37	36	6	1.89
1912	50	32	12	368	303	76	37	34	7	1.39
1913	47	36	7	346	243	38	36	30	12	1.09
1914	51	28	18	372	225	74	40	33	10	1.72
1915	47	27	13	337	203	56	39	35	8	1.55
1916	48	25	20	371	228	132	38	36	3	1.89
1917	47	23	16	328	188	67	34	30	8	2.30
1918	39	23	13	325	162	70	29	29	8	1.27
1919	39	20	14	290	147	51	29	27	7	1.49
1920	21	8	10	144	78	27	15	12	4	3.13
1921	35	17	14	264	143	92	32	25	1	3.51
1922	41	15	16	280	105	99	31	23	4	2.99
1923	43	17	12	262	130	69	35	18	3	3.54
1924	38	23	7	278	158	77	38	20	6	2.72
1925	30	20	7	229	108	78	29	16	3	3.07
1926	33	15	16	262	125	73	33	22	2	3.61
1927	18	5	6	108	48	26	15	7	1	5.10
TOTAL	802	416	279	5925	3508	1405	666	532	113	2.17

For sheer numbers, not many were better than Walter Johnson. He won 416 games, more than many pitchers are permitted to start. His long reach may have been the secret behind his blazing fastball.

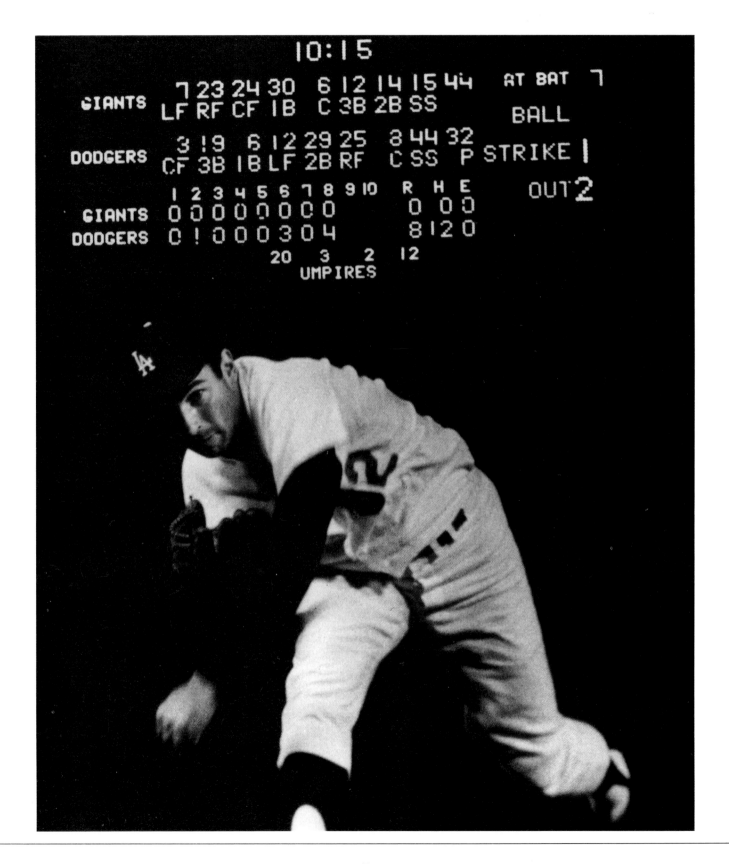

SANDY KOUFAX

Sandy Koufax was truly a blazing comet on the baseball horizon. He didn't have the longevity enjoyed by Cy Young or Walter Johnson, but when he was at his best, no one was finer.

With an average of 9.27 strikeouts per nine innings, Koufax remains one of only two pitchers to average more than one strikeout per inning.

For a period of six years, Sanford Koufax was as great a pitcher as has ever played the game. He was completely and utterly dominant.

Before 1961, the Dodgers' left-hander needed six seasons to find his control, to harness his pyrotechnic fastball and lethal curve. In 1966 his career was over, called because of arthritis. In between, Sandy Koufax combined all that raw power with superb control and set the record book on fire.

Those six seasons yielded a record 129-47 and five straight earned run average titles. Koufax threw four no-hitters in four consecutive years, something no one has yet equaled. He won the strikeout title four times and the Cy Young Award as the best pitcher in the majors three times. In particular, his 1963 and 1965 seasons were among the most brilliant in baseball history.

Koufax led the majors in strikeouts with 269 in 1961 and a year later topped the National League with an earned run average of 2.54. In 1963, it all came together. The 6-foot-2, 210-pound Brooklyn native had lost more games than he won (36-40) in his first six seasons in Brooklyn and then Los Angeles.

After going 18-13 in 1961 and 14-7 a year later, Koufax broke through with a 25-5 record in 1963. His earned run average was a formidable 1.88, he struck out 306 batters and

pitched 11 shutouts. Koufax was named the Most Valuable Player, but he deserved the award merely on the basis of his World Series performance. The Dodgers swept the New York Yankees, 4-0, chiefly because Koufax was impossible to hit. He pitched two complete game victories, allowing three earned runs and striking out 23 batters and walking only 3.

Koufax topped himself in 1965, winning 26 games and losing only 8 in 41 starts. His earned run average was 2.04, the strikeout total was a blinding 382, still a National League record. Put that in perspective by considering that the Mets' Dwight Gooden struck out 268 batters when he won the Cy Young Award in 1985. Koufax also posted a league-leading 27 complete games and eight shutouts. With the '65 World Series tied between the Dodgers and Minnesota at two-all, Koufax struck out 10 Twins and scattered four singles, leading the Dodgers to a 7-0 victory. In the seventh game he pitched his second consecutive shutout, throwing a three-hitter and recording another 10 strikeouts. In a total of 24 innings, Koufax struck out 29 batters and walked only 5. His earned run average was a scant .38.

His brilliance had its price, however. Arthritis of the left elbow forced Koufax to retire after the 1966 season, at age 31. He didn't post the career numbers of Walter Johnson or Cy Young, but for six fleeting seasons, Sandy Koufax was the pitcher of record.

As a child on the sand lot, Sandy Koufax could bat with the best of them. As he grew, though, he found his true calling: pitching. The ball even looked lethal in his hands.

His motion was a thing of beauty, fluid and awe-inspiring. Sadly, Koufax's magic was short lived.

S T A T S

YEAR	G	W	L	IP	SO	TBB	GS	CG	ShO	ERA
1955	12	2	2	42	30	28	5	2	2	3.02
1956	16	2	4	59	30	29	10	0	0	4.91
1957	34	5	4	104	122	51	13	2	0	3.88
1958	40	11	11	159	131	105	26	5	0	4.48
1959	35	8	6	153	173	92	23	6	1	4.05
1960	37	8	13	175	197	100	26	7	2	3.91
1961	42	18	13	256	269	96	35	15	2	3.52
1962	28	14	7	184	216	57	26	11	2	2.54
1963	40	25	5	311	306	58	40	20	11	1.88
1964	29	19	5	223	223	53	28	15	7	1.74
1965	43	26	8	336	382	71	41	27	8	2.04
1966	41	27	9	323	317	77	41	27	5	1.73
TOTAL	397	165	87	2325	2396	817	314	137	40	2.76

MICKEY MANTLE

Mickey Mantle was quick out of the batter's box for a home run hitter. An old football injury, however, forced him to take the bases slowly.

Mantle holds the World Series record of 18 career home runs.

In 1931, Mickey Charles Mantle was named after Mickey Cochrane, the great American League catcher of the time. His parents must have known something.

At 19, Mantle left Spavinaw, Oklahoma to play at Joplin, Missouri, where he hit .383 with 26 home runs and 123 runs batted in. That was Class C ball, but a year later Mantle tried to make the quantum leap to the New York Yankees. He opened the season in right field with a huge burden on his back: a number 6. The Babe himself had worn number 3, Lou Gehrig had number 4, and Joe DiMaggio was still gracing center field with number 5. Obviously, much was expected from this 5-foot-11, 195-pound phenom. When his average dipped to .260, Mantle was shipped down to Kansas City for six weeks of seasoning. On return, Mantle very quietly requested number 7.

Mantle possessed that rare combination of power and speed, and he could hit the ball farther and run faster than almost anyone. He hit 536 home runs in 18 years—and he did it from both sides of the plate. No switch-hitter ever had that kind of record. Mantle, despite his riveting speed, stole only 153 bases during his career. An old football injury developed into an arrested case of osteomyelitis, a bone infection in his right leg. And so, the Yankees rarely took chances with Mantle on the base paths.

In the 1951 World Series, Mantle tore knee cartilage when he stepped on the wooden lid of a drainpipe in right-center field. Oddly enough, the ball was hit by Willie Mays and caught by DiMaggio. His legs, weak to begin with, were never quite the same. Yet Mantle accomplished some fairly amazing things. Named Most Valuable Player three times, he won it back-to-back in 1956 and 1957. In those two years, Mantle averaged .358, hit 86 home runs, and drove in 224 runs.

In 1961, when Roger Maris eclipsed Babe Ruth's record with 61 home runs, Mantle was within two of Maris as late as September 5. Typically, failing health intervened and a virus took Mantle out of the race. Still, he hit 54 homers, a total surpassed by only five men.

In 1963, a year after he won his last MVP Award, Mantle ran into the wall in Baltimore as he tried to make a catch in center field, breaking a bone in his left foot and tearing another knee cartilage. He missed most of the season and was eventually moved to first base. Historians of the game often wonder what Mantle might have accomplished if he had been healthy throughout his career.

Sometimes, however, justice does prevail. In 1974, Mantle joined his namesake in the Hall of Fame.

Though he doesn't receive much credit for it, Mickey Mantle was a complete ballplayer. This shot, though, was staged for the camera.

S T A T S

YEAR	G	AB	H	2B	3B	HR	TB	R	RBI	BB	AVG
1951	96	341	91	11	5	13	151	61	65	43	.267
1952	142	549	171	37	7	23	291	94	87	75	.311
1953	127	461	136	24	3	21	229	105	92	79	.295
1954	146	543	163	17	12	27	285	129	102	102	.300
1955	147	517	158	25	11	37	316	121	99	113	.306
1956	150	533	188	22	5	52	376	132	130	112	.353
1957	144	474	173	28	6	34	315	121	94	146	.365
1958	150	519	158	21	1	42	307	127	97	129	.304
1959	144	541	154	23	4	31	278	104	75	94	.285
1960	153	527	145	17	6	40	294	119	94	111	.275
1961	153	514	163	16	6	54	353	132	128	126	.317
1962	123	377	121	15	1	30	228	96	89	122	.321
1963	65	172	54	8	0	15	107	40	35	40	.314
1964	143	465	141	25	2	35	275	92	111	99	.303
1965	122	361	92	12	1	19	163	44	46	73	.255
1966	108	333	96	12	1	23	179	40	56	57	.288
1967	144	440	108	17	0	22	191	63	55	107	.245
1968	144	435	103	14	1	18	173	57	54	106	.237
TOTAL	**2401**	**8102**	**2415**	**344**	**72**	**536**	**4511**	**1677**	**1509**	**1734**	**.298**

Willie Mays had it all. Size. Speed. Power. Grace. He was the prototypical baseball player.

WILLIE MAYS

Mays won 11 Gold Gloves as a center fielder for the Giants.

Perhaps no player so excited baseball quite the way the "Say Hey Kid" did in the 1950s and 1960s. Willie Howard Mays was electric. At the plate, on the bases, in the field—especially in the field.

He tore the minor leagues up after the New York Giants signed the 19-year-old in 1950. Mays passed quickly through Trenton and Minneapolis and was called up a year later when manager Leo Durocher needed a glove for the Polo Grounds' yawning center field. Although Mays failed to hit in his first 12 at-bats, Durocher wouldn't return him to the minors. He had seen the 5-foot-10, 170-pound Mays at work in the outfield. He could chase down anything that stayed in the park and had the arm strength to make a throw from wherever his fleet feet had taken him. His speed and instincts allowed him to play closer to the infield than most center fielders, so he saved Giants pitchers numerous singles.

Eventually, the hits began to come and the Giants, too, began to find themselves. They trailed the Brooklyn Dodgers by 13½ games on August 12, 1951, but won 37 of their final 44 games and caught the Dodgers at the wire. On October 3, Bobby Thomson's home run cleared the wall in left field and another baseball legend was born. Thus, the Giants won the National League pennant and Mays' modest contribution of 20 home runs and 68 runs

batted in undoubtedly helped. The Army prevented him from making much of an impact in 1952 or 1953, but the next year Mays began a terrific run of success.

In many ways, 1954 might have been his best season; it showed the world what was possible. Through 99 games, Mays had hit 36 home runs. Even in late June he had been far ahead of Babe Ruth's record pace, but the Giants were in a pennant race with the Dodgers and Braves and Durocher needed singles in greater regularity to win. Though Mays hit only five home runs over the last two months of the season, he raised his batting average to .345, a figure that led the majors. After the Giants swepts four games from Cleveland in the World Series, Mays was named the league's Most Valuable Player.

He hit 51 home runs the next season and in the following year stole 40 bases. There wasn't anything he couldn't do, as his staggering career statistics indicate: 3,283 hits, 6,066 total bases, 660 home runs, 1,903 runs batted in, 2,062 runs scored, 338 stolen bases.

As he grew older, Mays' power showed no signs of diminishing. Between the ages of thirty and forty, Mays averaged 35 home runs per season at Candlestick Park. In 1971, at the age of forty, Mays stole 23 bases, more than he had in ten years. Say Hey.

Even Willie Mays' failures were brilliant efforts. If he couldn't reach that ball in the gap, who could?

S T A T S

YEAR	G	AB	H	2B	3B	HR	TB	R	RBI	BB	AVG
1951	121	464	127	22	5	20	219	59	68	56	.274
1952	34	127	30	2	4	4	52	17	23	16	.236
1954	151	565	195	33	13	41	377	119	110	66	.345
1955	152	580	185	18	13	51	382	123	127	79	.319
1956	152	578	171	27	8	36	322	101	84	68	.296
1957	152	585	195	26	20	35	366	112	97	76	.333
1958	152	600	208	33	11	29	350	121	96	78	.347
1959	151	575	180	43	5	34	335	125	104	65	.313
1960	153	595	190	29	12	29	330	107	103	61	.319
1961	154	572	176	32	3	40	334	129	123	81	.308
1962	162	621	189	36	5	49	382	130	141	78	.304
1963	157	596	187	32	7	38	347	115	103	66	.314
1964	157	578	171	21	9	47	351	121	111	82	.296
1965	157	558	177	21	3	52	360	118	112	76	.317
1966	152	552	159	29	4	37	307	99	103	70	.288
1967	141	486	128	22	2	22	220	83	70	51	.263
1968	148	498	144	20	5	23	243	84	79	67	.289
1969	117	403	114	17	3	13	176	64	58	49	.283
1970	139	478	139	15	2	28	242	94	83	79	.291
1971	136	417	113	24	5	18	201	82	61	112	.271
1972	88	244	61	11	1	8	98	35	22	60	.250
1973	66	209	44	10	0	6	72	24	25	27	.211
TOTAL	2992	10881	3283	523	140	660	6066	2062	1903	1463	.302

Sometimes, the "Say Hey" kid just couldn't contain his enthusiasm. With Willie Mays, you always expected the unexpected and in most cases he delivered.

STAN MUSIAL

Stan Musial was nothing if not consistent. For 13 straight seasons, he had 183 hits or more.

Musial appeared in 24 All-Star games.

Like Babe Ruth, Stanley Frank Musial was once a pitcher. This was before he arrived in St. Louis, became "Stan the Man," and started hitting line drives all over the place.

He was born in Donora, Pennsylvania in 1920 and 20 years later found himself a 6-foot, 175-pound, left-handed pitcher scuffling along in Class C ball. He wasn't striking out any people and he switched to the outfield, getting the call up to the Cardinals in 1941. Musial's batting stance was a little strange; he looked like a moving corkscrew as he unleashed his body at the ball. But soon everyone knew something wonderful was at work as Musial managed 20 hits in 12 games that season. For the next 22 years (save one for the war effort in 1945), Musial moved into the starting lineup and never stopped hitting.

He wasn't a slugger, but a pure hitter who just seemed to hit doubles (725) at will. Only Tris Speaker and Pete Rose hit more and only Hank Aaron finished with more extra-base hits. The .300 batting mark is a cherished accomplishment, but Musial hit over .310 in 18 different seasons and won the National League batting title seven times.

Stamped with the hallmark of greatness, Musial withstood the test of time, producing quality in quantity. For a stretch in the 1940s, no one hit a baseball better. Musial won the Most Valuable Player Award in 1943, when he hit a league-leading .357, including 48 doubles and 20 triples. St. Louis reached the World Series but lost to the Yankees. Musial's numbers the next year were nearly as good (.347, 51 doubles, 14 triples) and the Cardinals eventually beat their cross-town rivals, the Browns, in the 1944 World Series. Musial's three hits in Game Four launched the Cardinals on a three-game winning streak.

Musial missed the 1945 season and, perhaps as a consequence, the Cardinals missed the World Series. Back the next year, he won the MVP Award a second time with a .365 average, 50 doubles and 20 triples—and St. Louis beat Boston in the 1946 World Series. In 1948, Musial hit .376, slugged .702 and put together a routine 46 doubles and 18 triples. He was named MVP again, for the third time in five seasons.

In 1952, Musial made his only major league appearance on the mound. He didn't allow a hit, nor did he get anyone out. That's why they made him a hitter.

Look at that swing. What were the St. Louis Cardinals thinking when they sent him out to the mound to pitch?

S T A T S

YEAR	G	AB	H	2B	3B	HR	TB	R	RBI	BB	AVG
1941	12	47	20	4	0	1	27	8	7	2	.426
1942	140	467	147	32	10	10	229	87	72	62	.315
1943	157	617	220	48	20	13	347	108	81	72	.357
1944	146	568	197	51	14	12	312	112	94	90	.347
1946	156	624	228	50	20	16	366	124	103	73	.365
1947	149	587	183	30	13	19	296	113	95	80	.312
1948	155	611	230	46	18	39	429	135	131	79	.376
1949	157	612	207	41	13	36	382	128	123	107	.338
1950	146	555	192	41	7	28	331	105	109	87	.346
1951	152	578	205	30	12	32	355	124	108	98	.355
1952	154	578	194	42	6	21	311	105	91	96	.336
1953	157	593	200	53	9	30	361	127	113	105	.337
1954	153	591	195	41	9	35	359	120	126	103	.330
1955	154	562	179	30	5	33	318	97	108	80	.319
1956	156	594	184	33	6	27	310	87	109	75	.310
1957	134	502	176	38	3	29	307	82	102	66	.351
1958	135	472	159	35	2	17	249	64	62	72	.337
1959	115	341	87	13	2	14	146	37	44	60	.255
1960	116	331	91	17	1	17	161	49	63	41	.275
1961	123	372	107	22	4	15	182	46	70	52	.288
1962	135	433	143	18	1	19	220	57	82	64	.330
1963	124	337	86	10	2	12	136	34	58	35	.255
TOTAL	3026	10972	3630	725	177	475	6134	1949	1951	1599	.331

BROOKS ROBINSON

Brooks Robinson successfully handled 8,902 of 9,165 chances at third base, for a major league fielding percentage record of .971.

It isn't often that a player makes a lasting impact on baseball. It is even rarer when he does it without a bat or a ball. Brooks Calbert Robinson was a glove man, the best third baseman the game has ever seen. He made defense fashionable in the modern era by winning 16 consecutive Gold Glove Awards as his position's best fielder.

Robinson played in more games (2,687), handled more chances (9,165), produced more assists (6,205), and was involved in more double plays (618) than any other third baseman. His career batting average of .267 is almost a moot point.

When he emerged from Little Rock, Arkansas in 1955, Robinson left in his wake a number of critics who claimed the 6-foot-1, 180-pounder wasn't fast enough to make the majors. Yet the Baltimore Orioles liked what they saw and called him up at the age of 18. Robinson produced only two hits in 22 at-bats and spent the next four years bounding between Baltimore and places like San Antonio and Vancouver. When he returned from the minor leagues for the last time on July 9, 1959, Robinson played in 97 percent of the Orioles' games over the next sixteen years.

And, contrary to perceptions, Robinson had a serviceable bat. The right-hander hit .303 in 1962 and .317 two years later, knocked in 100 runs or more twice, and hit 20 or more home runs six different times. Robinson's 268 career home runs were a record for American League third basemen at one time. His career League Championship Series is .348, which says something about his ability to deliver under duress. In 1964, he was the league's MVP.

It is the memory of his glove, though, that people cherish. In 1970, he carried the Orioles to a five-game World Series victory over the Cincinnati Reds. Baltimore won the first three games, its 17th in a row. In that third game, Robinson destroyed the spirit of the Reds' right-handed power hitters, reaching two sure hits down the line and pounding a two-run double. When Baltimore had prevailed, Robinson was named Most Valuable Player on the basis of his magnificent fielding performance, not to mention a .429 batting average, two home runs, and six runs batted in.

The end came in 1977. Robinson was 40 years old, battling Cleveland reliever Dave LaRoche. He was pinch-hitting for Larry Harlow in a tenth-inning game the Orioles trailed

5-3. With two men on base, he ran the count to three-and-two, fouled off several pitches, then hit the ball over the fence in left field. It was his last home run and one of baseball's more emotional moments.

STATS

YEAR	G	AB	H	2B	3B	HR	TB	R	RBI	BB	AVG
1955	6	22	2	0	0	0	2	0	1	0	.091
1956	15	44	10	4	0	1	17	5	1	1	.227
1957	50	117	28	6	1	2	42	13	14	7	.239
1958	145	463	110	16	3	3	141	31	32	31	.238
1959	88	313	89	15	2	4	120	29	24	17	.284
1960	152	595	175	27	9	14	262	74	88	35	.294
1961	163	668	192	38	7	7	265	89	61	47	.287
1962	162	634	192	29	9	23	308	77	86	42	.303
1963	161	589	148	26	4	11	215	67	67	46	.251
1964	163	612	194	35	3	28	319	82	118	51	.317
1965	144	559	166	25	2	18	249	81	80	47	.297
1966	157	620	167	35	2	23	275	91	100	56	.269
1967	158	610	164	25	5	22	265	88	77	54	.269
1968	162	608	154	36	6	17	253	65	75	44	.253
1969	156	598	140	21	3	23	236	73	84	56	.234
1970	158	608	168	31	4	18	261	84	94	53	.276
1971	156	589	160	21	1	20	243	67	92	63	.272
1972	153	556	139	23	2	8	190	48	64	43	.250
1973	155	549	141	17	2	9	189	53	72	55	.257
1974	153	553	159	27	0	7	207	46	59	56	.288
1975	144	482	97	15	1	6	132	50	53	44	.201
1976	71	218	46	8	2	3	67	16	11	8	.211
1977	24	47	7	2	0	1	12	3	4	4	.149
TOTAL	2896	10654	2848	482	68	268	4270	1232	1357	860	.267

Out of the frying pan and into the hole between third and shortstop—that was Brooks Robinson's forte.

PETE ROSE

For nine straight seasons, from 1965 to 1973, Rose batted better than .300.

He ran when others walked.

Critics said it wasn't necessary—not to mention downright arrogant—but this was merely Charlie Hustle's way of wearing his aggressive heart on his sleeve. Peter Edward Rose truly ran into the record books with elbows and dust flying everywhere.

Rose, a solid 5-foot-11, 200-pound switch-hitter, made hitting singles respectable in a sport where home runs are very much the main attraction. When he was finished, Rose had established searing career standards for future generations to contemplate: Most hits (4,256), games played (3,562), plate appearances (15,890), singles (3,215), and seasons with 200 or more hits (10).

Rose did everything with a little extra gusto, which is why he was still playing at age 45. In fact, 1986 was the first season in 24 that Rose did not play in 100 games, although he was also managing his Cincinnati Reds at the time. He did a good job, which is hardly surprising, considering Rose believed that giving the most of yourself was the only way to approach a task. Whether it was daring base running or playing the outfield, Rose, well, hustled. Invariably, he took the extra base or caught the ball that looked to be out of reach. People are surprised to hear that Rose is certifiably one of the best outfielders ever, based

on his lifetime fielding percentage of .991.

This, from the unfortunate young second baseman who at age 19 committed a league-leading 36 errors for Geneva of the New York-Pennsylvania League in 1960. Despite the bad fielding, Rose was promoted to the Florida State League's Tampa franchise. There, he led the league with 160 hits in 130 games, including 30 triples. Another year in Macon, Georgia prepared him for spring training in 1963.

While the rest of the players were going through the motions, Rose was hurtling all over the field. Mickey Mantle was moved to observe one day, "Look at Charlie Hustle." He didn't mean it kindly, but Rose took it as a compliment. He made the Reds team and was named the National League's Rookie of the Year for hitting .273. He hit .269 in 1964, which set the stage for a remarkable 15 seasons. Rose hit .300 or better for 14 of those years and produced more than 200 hits in 10 of them.

And on September 11, 1985, Rose found himself at Cincinnati's Riverfront Stadium staring out at San Diego's Eric Show. The 2-1 slider was inside and low, but Rose hacked at it and the ball bounced in front of left fielder Carmelo Martinez. It was career base hit 4,192 for Pete Rose which pushed him one past the great Ty Cobb. And he ran as fast as he could all the way to first base.

 *No player ever spent more time airborne than Pete Rose. The classic head-first slide was one of his trademarks.*

Efficiency was Pete Rose's greatest talent. He took his rather common resources and produced an uncommon body of baseball work.

S T A T S

YEAR	G	AB	H	2B	3B	HR	TB	R	RBI	BB	AVG
1963	157	623	170	25	9	6	231	101	41	55	.273
1964	136	516	139	13	2	4	168	64	34	36	.269
1965	162	670	209	35	11	11	299	117	81	69	.312
1966	156	654	205	38	5	16	301	97	70	37	.313
1967	148	585	176	32	8	12	260	86	76	56	.301
1968	149	626	210	42	6	10	294	94	49	56	.335
1969	156	627	218	33	11	16	321	120	82	88	.348
1970	159	649	205	37	9	15	305	120	52	73	.316
1971	160	632	192	27	4	13	266	86	44	68	.304
1972	154	645	198	31	11	6	269	107	57	73	.307
1973	160	680	230	36	8	5	297	115	64	65	.338
1974	163	652	185	45	7	3	253	110	51	106	.284
1975	162	662	210	47	4	7	286	112	74	89	.317
1976	162	665	215	42	6	10	299	130	63	86	.323
1977	162	655	204	38	7	9	283	95	64	66	.311
1978	159	655	198	51	3	7	276	103	52	62	.302
1979	163	628	208	40	5	4	270	90	59	95	.331
1980	162	655	185	42	1	1	232	95	64	66	.282
1981	107	431	140	18	5	0	168	73	33	46	.325
1982	162	634	172	25	4	3	214	80	54	66	.271
1983	151	493	121	14	3	0	141	52	45	52	.245
1984	121	374	107	15	2	0	126	43	34	40	.286
1985	119	405	107	12	2	2	129	60	46	86	.264
1986	72	237	52	8	2	0	64	15	25	30	.219
TOTAL	3562	14053	4256	746	135	160	5752	2165	1314	1566	.303

Always, Pete Rose studied the game, the count, the situation. It was this curiosity which led to his ascension to the Cincinnati Reds' manager.

BABE RUTH

Ruth has baseball's best home run/at-bats ratio, with a homer for every 11.76 at-bats. Hank Aaron, who broke his 714-homer mark, has a ratio of 16.38.

Rarely does one man come to personify an entire sport. It happened in baseball, though, in the form of George Herman Ruth, The Sultan of Swat, The Bambino. The Babe.

Ruth was born in Baltimore in 1895. At 19, just out of St. Mary's Industrial Home for Boys in Baltimore, he was purchased from the bankrupt Orioles by the Red Sox for $2,900. Ruth was hardly a heavy hitter at the time. His first season in the big leagues brought him exactly 10 at-bats (he got two hits, including a double), because Babe was a pitcher. The 6-foot-2, 215-pound left-hander was a good one, too. The next year, Ruth led the American League with 18 victories and only 8 losses—he also was permitted to bat 92 times, resulting in 29 hits, four of them home runs. Manager Rough Carrigan quickly discovered Ruth's ability with the bat and used him frequently as a left-handed pinch-hitter.

While the Red Sox were in the process of winning three World Series in four years, Ruth continued to flower as a hitter. In fact, when Boston capped its flurry with a victory over Chicago in six games, it was Ruth's last year of substance on the mound. Two World Series wins paled by comparison to the .300 average he fashioned in 317 at-bats over the regular season. His 11 home runs led the league. In 1919, his last year with the Red Sox, Ruth was 9-5 on the mound and batted .322 at the plate. He also hit 29 home runs to lead the league.

That was enough to set the New York Yankees salivating. When Boston owner Harry Frazee found himself in a financial bind, he shipped Ruth to New York in exchange for $125,000 in cash and a $300,000 loan. Ruth pitched in only five more games the rest of his career and, not surprisingly, won all of them.

Responding immediately to his new environment, Ruth hit 54 homers in 1920. He added 59 more the next season, scored 177 runs and drove in 171. Ruth walked 144 times that year, something he was to do better than anyone in baseball. Such was his eye at the plate and the respect he commanded.

Mere numbers fail to adequately describe the impact Ruth had on baseball. He is still the all-time leader in slugging average (.690), home run percentage (8.5), and bases on balls (2,056). When Hank Aaron passed Ruth's record 714 home runs in 1974, the sports world watched, not quite sure how to feel. He remains the number two man, behind Aaron, in home runs and runs batted in. And only Ty Cobb crossed the plate more times than Ruth.

It might have happened differently. Ruth might have become one of the best pitchers in history as his 94-46 lifetime record suggests. He settled for being the best slugger.

Here he is, the stuff of legends. Babe Ruth is a rarity—he lived up to all those amazing stories told about him.

Even during his career, Babe Ruth transcended the game. And, after he retired, his fame grew even greater.

S T A T S

YEAR	G	AB	H	2B	3B	HR	TB	R	RBI	BB	AVG
1914	5	10	2	1	0	0	3	1	0	0	.200
1915	42	92	29	10	1	4	53	16	20	9	.315
1916	67	136	37	5	3	3	57	18	16	10	.272
1917	52	123	40	6	3	2	58	14	10	12	.325
1918	95	317	95	26	11	11	176	50	64	57	.300
1919	130	432	139	34	12	29	284	103	112	101	.322
1920	142	458	172	36	9	54	388	158	137	148	.376
1921	152	540	204	44	16	59	457	177	171	144	.378
1922	110	406	128	24	8	35	273	94	99	84	.315
1923	152	522	205	45	13	41	399	151	131	170	.393
1924	153	529	200	39	7	46	391	143	121	142	.378
1925	98	359	104	12	2	25	195	61	66	59	.290
1926	152	495	184	30	5	47	365	139	145	144	.372
1927	151	540	192	29	8	60	417	158	164	138	.356
1928	154	536	173	29	8	54	380	163	142	135	.323
1929	135	499	172	26	6	46	348	121	154	72	.345
1930	145	518	186	28	9	49	379	150	153	136	.359
1931	145	534	199	31	3	46	374	149	163	128	.373
1932	133	457	156	13	5	41	302	120	137	130	.341
1933	137	459	138	21	3	34	267	97	103	114	.301
1934	125	365	105	17	4	22	196	78	84	103	.288
1935	28	72	13	0	0	6	31	13	12	20	.181
TOTAL	2503	8399	2873	506	136	714	5793	2174	2204	2056	.342

© John Zimmerman/FPG Intl.

NOLAN RYAN

Ryan struck out 19 batters in a game four different times.

Smoke, pure smoke. That is the essence of Lynn Nolan Ryan. Nobody did it better, no one ever threw faster than Ryan. His fastball was clocked at 100.8 miles an hour one game in 1974, but the sight of opposing batters leaving the batter's box in a daze suggests Ryan is faster still.

For sheer firepower, the 6-foot-2, 200-pound right-hander is baseball's best. Through 1986, at age 40, Ryan had struck out 4,277 batters, the all-time record. When he was throwing strikes—his total of 2,268 bases on balls is also a record—Ryan was just about impossible to hit. The numbers back him up: On September 26, 1981, Ryan became the first man in history to throw *five* no-hitters. And four of them came in a span of three years. The near-misses are just as impressive. Ryan has thrown nine one-hitters, 18 two-hitters and 26 three-hitters.

He was born in Refugio, Texas and 18 years later, in 1965, Ryan was an eighth-round draft choice of the New York Mets. In 1966, Ryan led the Western Carolina League with 272 strikeouts and a 17-2 record. From that single-A club, he made the jump all the way to the majors in a season's time. Ryan spent four full seasons with the Mets, including 1969's impossible championship season. In 1971, he was traded to the California Angels along with three other players in exchange for Jim Fregosi. What followed was similarly amazin'.

In his eight years with the Angels, Ryan led the American League seven times in strikeouts. He averaged 302 Ks per year over that time. Ryan also led the league in bases on balls in six of those eight years, which is one reason his average per-year record through 1986 was 13-12.

Yet of his 253 career victories, 54 were shutouts. In addition to fanning 4,277 batters, Ryan had the major league's best strikeout ratio. For every nine innings he pitched, Ryan struck out more than nine batters. Sandy Koufax was the only other pitcher who could claim that distinction.

Through 1986, he had reached double figures in strikeouts 162 times, a major-league record. How incredible is that? Imagine Ryan starting the opener and striking out at least 10 batters in every game of the season. Imagine that.

STATS

YEAR	G	W	L	IP	SO	TBB	GS	CG	ShO	ERA
1966	2	0	1	3	6	3	1	0	0	15.00
1968	21	6	9	134	133	75	18	3	0	3.09
1969	25	6	3	89	92	53	10	2	0	3.53
1970	27	7	11	132	125	97	19	5	2	3.41
1971	30	10	14	152	137	116	26	3	0	3.97
1972	39	19	16	284	329	157	39	20	9	2.28
1973	41	21	16	326	383	162	39	26	4	2.87
1974	42	22	16	333	367	202	41	26	3	2.89
1975	28	14	12	198	186	132	28	10	5	3.45
1976	39	17	18	284	327	183	39	21	7	3.36
1977	37	19	16	299	341	204	37	22	4	2.77
1978	31	10	13	235	260	148	31	14	3	2.71
1979	34	16	14	223	223	114	34	17	5	3.59
1980	35	11	10	234	200	98	35	4	2	3.35
1981	21	11	5	149	140	68	21	5	3	1.69
1982	35	16	12	250	245	109	35	10	3	3.16
1983	29	14	9	196	183	101	29	5	2	2.98
1984	30	12	11	184	197	69	30	5	2	3.04
1985	35	10	12	232	209	95	35	4	0	3.80
1986	30	12	8	178	194	82	30	1	0	3.34
TOTAL	611	253	226	4115	4277	2268	577	203	54	3.15

Even at the age of 40, Nolan Ryan had an extremely live arm. His fastball struck panic in the hearts of hitters everywhere.

With his bat (35 homers or more for 12 seasons) or his glove (10 Gold Gloves), Mike Schmidt could beat you.

MIKE SCHMIDT

Schmidt has led the National League in home runs eight different times.

When they finally vote Michael Jack Schmidt into baseball's Hall of Fame, he will probably be one of the game's all-time greats. As of 1987, the numbers left room for no other conclusion.

Schmidt hit his 500th home run early in his 15th season. Hank Aaron, whose 755 career homers are the standard, had 510 through 15 years. Only Babe Ruth, Jimmie Foxx, Harmon Killebrew, and Willie McCovey reached 400 home runs in fewer at-bats.

At 37, Mike Schmidt found himself in distinguished historical company. Through 14 seasons, he was one of seven men in baseball history to hit 30 home runs and knock in 100 runs each year. Likewise, he had 12 seasons with 35 homers or more, a figure surpassed only by Ruth and Aaron, and they played 22 and 23 seasons, respectively. Schmidt also had achieved the major league's fourth-best career home run ratio (14.73), after Ruth, Killebrew and Ralph Kiner.

Through 1986, the 6-foot-2, 203-pound third baseman had already been named the National League's Most Valuable Player three times, including 1980 and 1981. Only Stan Musial and Roy Campanella equaled that feat. Schmidt had been selected to play in 10 All-Star games and won 10 Gold Gloves for fielding excellence, another league record.

He was born in Dayton, Ohio and eventually earned a degree in business administration from Ohio University in 1971. The Philadelphia Phillies assigned him to their Reading club, where Schmidt batted .211 and hit eight home runs in 74 games. At Eugene the next year, Schmidt hiked his average to .291 (despite 145 strikeouts) and was called up by the Phillies late in the season. He hit one homer in 34 at-bats, a rough start that was underlined by his first full season in 1973. Schmidt batted .196 and hit 18 home runs in 132 games. From that point, Schmidt failed to hit at least 30 home runs in a season only once.

From 1974 to 1977, Schmidt averaged 38 home runs and 105 runs batted in. He led the National League in strikeouts three times over that span, but that is the traditional price sluggers pay for their awesome power. In 1976, Schmidt hit four consecutive homers against the Chicago Cubs at Wrigley Field. Through 1986, he had 39 two-homer games.

In 1980, Schmidt led the league with a career-high 48 home runs and 121 runs batted in. In the World Series against the Kansas City Royals, he was named Most Valuable Player on the strength of his .381 batting average, 2 home runs, and 7 runs batted in. In 1986, Schmidt again led the league in home runs (37) and runs batted in (119). Where he'll stop nobody knows.

S T A T S

YEAR	G	AB	H	2B	3B	HR	TB	R	RBI	BB	AVG
1972	13	34	7	0	0	1	10	2	3	5	.206
1973	132	367	72	11	0	18	137	43	52	62	.196
1974	162	568	160	28	7	36	310	108	116	106	.282
1975	158	562	140	34	3	38	294	93	95	101	.249
1976	160	584	153	31	4	38	306	112	107	100	.262
1977	154	544	149	27	11	38	312	114	101	104	.274
1978	145	513	129	27	2	21	223	93	78	91	.251
1979	160	541	137	25	4	45	305	109	114	120	.253
1980	150	548	157	25	8	48	342	104	121	89	.286
1981	102	354	112	19	2	31	228	78	91	73	.316
1982	148	514	144	26	3	35	281	108	87	107	.280
1983	154	534	136	16	4	40	280	104	109	128	.255
1984	151	528	146	23	3	36	283	93	106	92	.277
1985	158	549	152	31	5	33	292	89	93	87	.277
1986	160	552	160	29	1	37	302	97	119	89	.290
TOTAL	2107	7292	1954	352	57	495	3905	1347	1392	1354	.268

BASEBALL
LEGENDS
The Players

When people remember the 1969 Mets,
they think of Tom Terrific on the mound
and the wonders he created.

TOM SEAVER

For nine consecutive seasons, from 1968 to 1976, Seaver struck out more than 200 batters per year, a major-league record.

When the Atlanta Braves tried to sign Tom Seaver out of Fresno City College in 1965, then-Commissioner William Eckert nullified the contract because a reported $40,000 signing bonus violated the school's rules. As a result, four teams put their names in a hat for Seaver and the pitiful New York Mets, who had averaged 113 losses for three seasons, finally won something: a pitcher. It wasn't long before they won the whole thing.

When George Thomas Seaver entered professional baseball he wasn't yet known as "Tom Terrific," but the 6-foot, 210-pound right-hander clearly was something special. He spent the 1966 season in Jacksonville, then stepped into the breach. Though the Mets lost 101 games in 1967, Seaver somehow managed 16 victories and was named the National League's Rookie of the Year. In the process, Seaver rewrote the Mets' pitching record book. He improved in virtually every category the next year, compiling a 16-12 record that only began to suggest the things to come.

The Mets, who were 73-89 in 1968, stunned the baseball world with a 100-62 record in 1969. Amazin' wasn't the word for it. They trailed the Chicago Cubs at one time by 9½ games, but rode Seaver's arm to the Eastern Division title. In early September with the season on the line, Seaver threw a one-hitter at the Cubs—Jimmy Qualls' ninth-inning single ruined a perfect game. The Mets won going away, by eight games, and Seaver's pitching was the reason: he finished with a 25-7 record, 208 strikeouts, an earned run average of 2.21. The World Series victory over Baltimore was almost anti-climactic.

In 1970, Seaver led the league with 283 strikeouts and duplicated the feat five times in seven years. On April 22, 1970, Seaver struck out 19 San Diego Padres, including the last 10 in a row, setting a major-league record. He established another major-league mark of ten seasons with 200 or more strikeouts. When he left the National League in 1984, Seaver owned the league record for lowest career earned run average (2.73) for a 200-game winner and the most strikeouts (3,272) by a right-handed pitcher.

His consistency was frightening. Seaver produced winning records in his first 15 consecutive seasons and won 311 games when he finished up with Boston in 1986. A strikeout total of 3,640 placed him third on the all-time list behind Nolan Ryan and Steve Carlton.

And in his last official season, 1986, Seaver wanted to play for a team within a few hours of his Connecticut home. It was a right he was due, for he had achieved everything baseball had to offer. Seaver eventually chose Boston and helped the Red Sox to the World Series 20 years after the Mets had plucked their fortunes from a fedora.

Then in 1987, the Mets appealed to their former ace when injuries decimated the pitching staff. Seaver signed a contract and agreed to try to pitch his way back into form. It never happened. "Baseball is a young man's game," said Seaver, now 40 years old. "And I didn't feel like I could contribute the way I wanted to."

It was vintage Seaver, a candid appraisal of the facts in hand. His contributions will one day be found in Cooperstown, New York.

				S	T	A	T	S		
YEAR	G	W	L	IP	SO	TBB	GS	CG	ShO	ERA
1967	35	16	13	251	170	78	34	18	2	2.76
1968	36	16	12	278	205	48	35	14	5	2.20
1969	36	25	7	273	208	82	35	18	5	2.21
1970	37	18	12	291	283	83	36	19	2	2.81
1971	36	20	10	286	289	61	35	21	4	1.76
1972	35	21	12	262	249	77	35	13	3	2.92
1973	36	19	10	290	251	64	36	18	3	2.08
1974	32	11	11	236	201	75	32	12	5	3.20
1975	36	22	9	280	243	88	36	15	5	2.38
1976	35	14	11	271	235	77	34	13	5	2.59
1977	33	21	6	261	196	66	33	19	7	2.59
1978	36	16	14	260	226	89	36	8	1	2.87
1979	32	16	6	215	131	61	32	9	5	3.14
1980	26	10	8	168	101	59	26	5	1	3.64
1981	23	14	2	166	87	66	23	6	1	2.55
1982	21	5	13	111	62	44	21	0	0	5.50
1983	34	9	14	231	135	86	34	5	2	3.55
1984	34	15	11	237	131	61	33	10	4	3.95
1985	35	16	11	240	134	69	33	6	1	3.17
1986	28	7	13	176	103	56	28	2	0	4.03
TOTAL	656	311	205	4783	3640	1390	647	231	61	2.86

HONUS WAGNER

Wagner hit well over .300 in each of his first 17 seasons in the major leagues.

Just who is baseball's greatest player? Even with a roster that included Babe Ruth and Ty Cobb, many would choose "The Flying Dutchman," John Honus Wagner. John McGraw, the legendary manager of the New York Giants for thirty years, insisted "Wagner was the best." Go ahead and argue with that.

There can be no argument that Honus Wagner was the quintessential "complete" player. Think of a prototypical shortstop today and one visualizes an Ozzie Smith, a graceful, spider-like player with a glove as big as his strike zone. Wagner was 5-foot-11, and a substantial 200 pounds. He did not look like a shortstop; in fact, he bounced around the outfield until manager Fred Clarke moved him to shortstop in 1901. But Wagner had huge hands—reaching for some tobacco one day at first base, his hand became stuck in his back pocket and eventually had to be cut free. Wagner's long arms gave him an uncommon range; he seemed to get to everything. Wagner had a strong arm and like most good shortstops, could throw from any position on the field. It was the same way with batting— he could hit any one at any time. To be sure, this was not a typical shortstop.

Wagner was a right-hander who, curiously, gripped the bat in the same fashion as Cobb, with his hands held a few inches apart. Just as Cobb terrorized the American League, so Wagner played above everybody in the National League, with the Pittsburgh Pirates for the last 18 years of his career. He broke in with Louisville in 1897, then moved to Pittsburgh with the franchise in 1900.

Wagner won eight National League batting titles, including four in a row, from 1906 to 1909. He averaged .346 over that period and helped defeat Cobb and the Detroit Tigers in the World Series of 1909 in the first season at Forbes Field. His consistent production, in terms of runs scored and batted in, was phenomenal. In a 21-year career, Wagner averaged 83 runs and 82 RBIs per year. His career average was .329. He also finished with 720 stolen bases and led the league five times in that category.

Quite simply, Wagner got the most from his talent. He preyed on mistakes by opposing pitchers. Like Joe Medwick, he was a classic "bad ball" hitter. The results, more often than not, were undeniably good.

Over a career that spanned 21 seasons, Honus Wagner averaged .329 at the plate and threw some pretty mean leather at shortstop.

S T A T S

YEAR	G	AB	H	2B	3B	HR	TB	R	RBI	BB	AVG
1897	61	241	83	17	4	2	114	38	39	15	.344
1898	151	591	180	31	4	10	249	80	105	31	.305
1899	147	571	197	47	13	7	291	102	113	40	.345
1900	135	528	201	45	22	4	302	107	100	41	.381
1901	141	556	196	39	10	6	273	100	126	53	.353
1902	137	538	177	33	16	3	251	105	91	43	.329
1903	129	512	182	30	19	5	265	97	101	44	.355
1904	132	490	171	44	14	4	255	97	75	59	.349
1905	147	548	199	32	14	6	277	114	101	54	.363
1906	142	516	175	38	9	2	237	103	71	58	.339
1907	142	515	180	38	14	6	264	98	82	46	.350
1908	151	568	201	39	19	10	308	100	109	54	.354
1909	137	495	168	39	10	5	242	92	100	66	.339
1910	150	556	178	34	8	4	240	90	81	59	.320
1911	130	473	158	23	16	9	240	87	89	67	.334
1912	145	558	181	35	20	7	277	91	102	59	.324
1913	114	413	124	18	4	3	159	51	56	26	.300
1914	150	552	139	15	9	1	175	60	50	51	.252
1915	151	566	155	32	17	6	239	68	78	39	.274
1916	123	432	124	15	9	1	160	45	39	34	.287
1917	74	230	61	7	1	0	70	15	24	24	.265
TOTAL	**2789**	**10449**	**3430**	**651**	**252**	**101**	**4888**	**1740**	**1732**	**963**	**.329**

TED WILLIAMS

*The science of hitting was Ted Williams'
specialty. The instrument of the terror
he wrought was a simple wooden bat.*

Williams led the American League in bases on balls for six straight seasons he appeared in, averaging 149 over that time.

He was the consummate craftsman, a man who mastered the science and intimate subtleties of the strike zone, perhaps better than anyone before or since. So keen was the batting eye of Theodore Samuel Williams that if he took a pitch, umpires invariably called it a ball.

Williams, 6-foot-3 and only 160 pounds as a rookie out of San Diego, torched the major leagues in 1939 when he arrived in Boston. He led the American League in runs batted in with 145 (the best total ever for a rookie), hit .327, finished second in doubles (44), and third in home runs (31) with the second-highest rookie totals in history, and drew 107 walks, another first-year record. And then, against all odds, the left fielder raised the level of his overall game.

In 1941, Joe DiMaggio made the headlines with a 56-game hitting streak, but during the same period, "The Splendid Splinter" outhit DiMaggio .412 to .408. Williams produced 185 hits that season in 456 official at-bats, and that translated to a .406 average. No one has reached the .400 plateau since. Like DiMaggio's streak, it is a standard against which the best players are measured.

In the All-Star game that year, Williams hit a dramatic three-run home run with two out

in the ninth off Claude Passeau of the National League. The American League won, 7-5, and Williams' greatness had been certified in a game that offered baseball's crème de la crème.

That .406 resulted in Williams' first batting title, but he would win five more. He won four home run titles and two triple crowns, in 1942 and 1947. Nine times, Williams led the league in slugging percentage. His place in baseball history is secure; Williams is among the career leaders in batting average, home runs, runs batted in, slugging percentage, and walks. This seems remarkable considering he missed nearly five full seasons due to military service and two major injuries.

Williams never seemed to lose the touch. In 1957, at 39, he batted .388 to lead the league and hit 38 home runs. The next year, his .328 average was again the best. In 1960, Williams appeared in 113 games for the Red Sox. He had never been a particular favorite of the fans there, who thought he was arrogant; Williams merely spoke the truth of his abilities. He hit 29 home runs in that farewell season, at the age of 42. The last came, appropriately, in his final game. And even Boston's stubborn fans had to rise to their feet in tribute. They knew they had seen a spectacular closing to a spectacular career.

YEAR	G	AB	H	2B	3B	HR	TB	R	RBI	BB	AVG
1939	149	565	185	44	11	31	344	131	145	107	.327
1940	144	561	193	43	14	23	333	134	113	96	.344
1941	143	456	185	33	3	37	335	135	120	145	.406
1942	150	522	186	34	5	36	338	141	137	145	.356
1946	150	514	176	37	8	38	343	142	123	156	.342
1947	156	528	181	40	9	32	335	125	114	162	.343
1948	137	509	188	44	3	25	313	124	127	126	.369
1949	155	566	194	39	3	43	368	150	159	162	.343
1950	89	334	106	24	1	26	216	82	97	82	.317
1951	148	531	169	28	4	30	295	109	126	144	.318
1952	6	10	4	0	1	1	9	2	3	2	.400
1953	37	91	37	6	0	13	82	17	34	19	.407
1954	117	386	133	23	1	29	245	93	89	136	.345
1955	98	320	114	21	3	28	225	77	83	91	.356
1956	136	400	138	28	2	24	242	71	82	102	.345
1957	132	420	163	28	1	38	307	96	87	119	.388
1958	129	411	135	23	2	26	240	81	85	98	.328
1959	103	272	69	15	0	10	114	32	43	52	.254
1960	113	310	98	15	0	29	200	56	72	75	.316
TOTAL	2292	7706	2654	525	71	521	4884	1798	1839	2019	.344

He didn't look for accolades—and the Fenway Park crowds rarely offered them—but Ted Williams was one of the game's most consistently brilliant performers.

Quite simply, Cy Young is the standard against which all pitchers are measured. His 511 career victories may never be equaled.

CY YOUNG

Young won more than 30 games five times in his 22-year career.

Commissioner of Baseball Ford Frick had a problem in 1956. He was concerned that voters for the Most Valuable Player awards tended to choose only every-day players, overlooking pitchers who took the mound every four or five days. Frick eventually concluded that a separate award should be created. Now, what to name it?

One name loomed above all others. Cy Young's 511 career victories were easily the highest total in baseball history, and made Frick's choice an easy one. Now, the Cy Young Award is voted to the best pitcher in each league. And with good reason.

Denton True "Cy" Young was born in Gilmore, Ohio in 1867. Twenty-three years later, the strapping 6-foot-2, 210 pound right-hander went 9-7 for Cleveland of the National League. In 1891, he won 27 games and won more than 20 games each season for fourteen consecutive years. During that span he won 395 games, more than anyone managed in a career, with the exception of Walter Johnson. That works out to an average per-season record of 28-15.

Of course, today's critics say that Young's achievements must be viewed with cynicism, suggesting that the conditions of play back in 1890 were too different to permit meaningful comparison. In 1903, when major league baseball stabilized into its present form, Young was already 36 years old. Still, he put together seasons of 28-9 and 26-16. A few years later, Young won 22 games in 1907 and 21 in 1908—at the age of 41.

He proved himself again and again. Young remains baseball's only 200—game winner in both the National and American leagues. He won 20 games or more sixteen times and Young's 36 victories in 1892 came from 49 starting opportunities. His 35-win season in 1895 represented more than half of Cleveland's victories. Young lost only 10 games that year.

Overall, there were two no-hitters and on one improbable day, a perfect game against the Athletics in 1904 when he pitched 24 consecutive hitless innings. Imagine that. Young appeared in the very first World Series in 1903 and won two of three games.

Yet, the arguments endure. Young was clearly ahead of his time. Is there evidence that he wouldn't have dominated today's game? No. And as each new hurling phenom blazes across our consciousness of the national pastime, remember the standard against which he is historically judged. If he is acclaimed as the best for an entire season, he wins the Cy Young Award.

S T A T S

YEAR	G	W	L	IP	SO	TBB	GS	CG	ShO	ERA
1890	17	9	7	148	39	30	16	16	0	3.47
1891	55	27	20	424	147	140	46	43	0	2.85
1892	53	36	11	453	168	118	49	48	9	1.93
1893	53	32	16	423	102	103	46	42	1	3.36
1894	52	25	22	409	108	106	47	44	2	3.94
1895	47	35	10	370	121	75	40	36	4	3.24
1896	51	29	16	414	140	62	46	42	5	3.24
1897	46	21	18	335	88	49	38	35	2	3.79
1898	46	25	14	378	101	41	41	40	1	2.53
1899	44	26	15	369	111	44	42	40	4	2.58
1900	41	20	18	321	115	36	35	32	4	3.00
1901	43	33	10	371	158	37	41	38	5	1.62
1902	45	32	10	385	160	53	43	41	3	2.15
1903	40	28	10	342	176	37	35	34	7	2.08
1904	43	26	16	380	200	29	41	40	10	1.97
1905	38	18	19	321	210	30	34	32	5	1.82
1906	39	13	21	288	140	25	34	28	0	3.19
1907	43	22	15	343	147	51	37	33	6	1.99
1908	36	21	11	299	150	37	33	30	3	1.26
1909	35	19	15	295	109	59	34	30	3	2.26
1910	21	7	10	163	58	27	20	14	1	2.53
1911	18	7	9	126	55	28	18	12	2	3.78
TOTAL	**906**	**511**	**313**	**7357**	**2803**	**1217**	**816**	**750**	**77**	**2.63**

Grab a pencil, get your scorecard here. Those scribbles you're making might be a part of history some day.

Two

The Games

When the National Association of Professional Baseball Players was formed in 1871, nine teams (including the Fort Wayne Kekiongas, the Rockford Forest Citys, the Washington Olympics, and the Boston Red Stockings) staked a $10 entry fee on the future. The Philadelphia Athletics won the initial championship with a 22-7 record.

These days, 26 teams play 162 games each season, most of which are forgotten as soon as they are played. A handful endure. Watch the Yankees' Don Larsen throw a perfect game at the Brooklyn Dodgers in 1956; agonize three years later as Pittsburgh's Harvey Haddix pitches 12 perfect innings—only to lose to the Milwaukee Braves in the 13th. Witness the magnitude of the epic 26-inning game that wouldn't end between the Boston Braves and Brooklyn Robins in 1920. Understand that the frenetic sixth game of the 1986 World Series may be remembered just as fondly by those who write history. And how does one quantify the impact of one Jackie Robinson when he broke into the Brooklyn Dodgers' lineup in 1947?

You don't—you just enjoy games like that and commit them to memory.

*The first man to greet Don Larsen after
his spellbinding effort against the
Dodgers was catcher Yogi Berra.*

Don Larsen's Perfect Game

Before the start of the 1956 World Series, it must have been difficult to guess who might emerge as the Series hero, the person who would be remembered long after the games were over. After all, talent was everywhere: the Yankees had Mickey Mantle, Yogi Berra, Elston Howard, and Whitey Ford; the Dodgers boasted Pee Wee Reese, Roy Campanella, Gil Hodges, Duke Snider, and Jackie Robinson, who was playing his last season. How then, did a nondescript right-hand pitcher make such improbable history at Yankee Stadium on October 8, 1956?

Good question. Don Larsen, 27, hadn't exactly torn up the major leagues in the previous four years. In fact, he had led the American League with 21 losses (to go with just 3 victories) two seasons earlier and carried a career record of 30-40 into the Series, having played for three teams in four years. When Larsen jeopardized a six-run lead by walking four Dodgers and allowing a base hit, he was yanked by manager Casey Stengel in the second inning of Game Two.

Still, Larsen was handed the ball three days later with the World Series tied at two games apiece. He struck out leadoff hitter Junior Gilliam looking with a curveball on the low inside corner. Reese ran the count to three and two and took another called third strike; he was the only Dodger who would see three balls that day. Snider lined to right and Larsen was out of the inning. And, against all kinds of odds, it went that way for nine innings.

The crowd of 64,519 grew louder as each inning passed. Using a no-windup delivery, the 6-foot-4, 215-pounder took a 2-0 lead into the eighth and set the Dodgers down in order. When he came to bat in the bottom half of the inning, he received a standing ovation.

The last three outs were difficult: right fielder Carl Furillo flied to right after fouling off four pitches, Campanella hit a long drive down the left field line foul before grounding to second base. Nervously, Larsen pitched to pinch-hitter Dale Mitchell, who was batting for Maglie. With the count two and one, Larsen loosed a fastball and Mitchell cocked his bat only to let the pitch go. Umpire Babe Pinelli, who didn't see the ball almost until it was in Berra's mitt, called the pitch, on the outside part of the plate, waist-high, a strike.

Larsen had thrown 97 pitches, gotten 27 outs, and not allowed a hit or a base on balls. For a single day, he was utterly perfect. It remains to this day the only perfect game thrown in World Series competition and one of the greatest pitching performances in history. And Larsen never recaptured that brief era of magic. He won three more World Series games for the Yankees and San Francisco Giants, but after that game, Larsen went on to play for four more teams, running his major league total to seven. And after that perfect game, Larsen was exactly a .500 pitcher.

He looked a little lean in that baggy
Dodgers uniform, but Jackie Robinson
eventually filled out. With help from
Branch Rickey, he changed the game
that he loved forever.

Jackie Robinson's First Game

In 1947 the Civil Rights Bill was still a quarter century away and equality was nonexistent, especially in baseball. Adrian "Cap" Anson and others like him, including baseball commissioner Kenesaw Mountain Landis, had conspired to keep the black man out of baseball. But when Albert B. "Happy" Chandler became commissioner, the winds of change started to ruffle the grand old game. "If a black can make it in Okinawa and go to Guadalcanal," Chandler reasoned, "he can make it in baseball."

Branch Rickey, the man who built the first successful farm system for St. Louis, tended to agree with Chandler. In 1945, he sent Brooklyn Dodgers scout Clyde Sukeforth on a mission to find Jack Roosevelt Robinson, a shortstop of some repute with the Kansas City Monarchs. Robinson was summoned to Rickey's office. "Jack, I've been looking for a great colored ballplayer, but I need more than a great player. I need a man who will accept insults, take abuse—in a word, carry the flag for his race."

This, Robinson did. Two years later, after leading Montreal to the 1946 Little World Series with a .349 batting average, Robinson was ready for the majors. But were the majors ready for him? On April 15, 1947, the world found out.

The Dodgers played the Boston Braves at Ebbets Field. Robinson, a second baseman by trade, played first that day. His first three at-bats resulted in outs. But in the seventh inning, he laid down a sacrifice bunt and took second base when the throw bounced off his shoulder into right field. Pete Reiser's single brought Robinson home with the winning run. It hardly mattered. What was important was that the color line had at last been broken. Robinson would go on to average .311 for ten seasons and ultimately reach the Hall of Fame.

And while baseball missed out on Josh Gibson and the best years of Satchel Paige, Robinson made it possible for players like Willie Mays to play in the major leagues. That was his legacy.

Muddy Ruel could scarcely believe his eyes: the ball took a strange hop past third baseman Fred Lindstrom and found its way into left field.

From left to right, Fred Lieb, Nick Altrock, Ty Cobb, Babe Ruth, John McGraw, Walter Johnson, George Sisler, and Christy Walsh pose just prior to the seventh game of the 1924 World Series—a game whose outcome was determined by a small pebble.

The Pebble Game

The 1924 World Series had been reduced to a single game, a contest that will be remembered as one of baseball's most unusual victories.

The Washington Senators and the New York Giants had split six games. On this October 10, they would finally decide the issue at Washington's Griffith Stadium. The Senators were trailing 3-1 when second baseman and manager Bucky Harris chopped a ball down the third base line with the bases loaded in the eighth inning. As New York third baseman Fred Lindstrom prepared to reel the bounding ball in, it skipped madly off a pebble and bounced over his head into left field. Thus, the game was tied at three.

Harris then called on his old warrior, Walter Johnson, to pitch the ninth. Now 37, Johnson had lost the opener in 12 innings (his first Series appearance in an eighteen-year career) despite striking out 12 batters. He teetered on the brink for four breathless innings, leaving men on base in every frame—including Frankie Frisch, who opened the ninth with a triple—but escaped unscathed.

It looked like the game was headed for the thirteenth inning, when Washington's leadoff hitter, Ralph Miller, grounded out and Muddy Ruel all but missed an offering from the Giants' Jack Bentley, hitting a little pop foul behind the plate, which catcher Hank Gowdy dropped when he tripped over his mask. Ruel promptly doubled past third and Johnson himself stepped to the plate. Again, fortune found the Senators as Johnson's bounding ball to shortstop was mismanaged by Travis Jackson. Earl McNeely came up with runners at first and second and laced a Bentley pitch down the third base line. Some have suggested that Lindstrom, a rookie, backed up on the ball and allowed it an extra hop. In any case, the ball hit a pebble or a clump of dirt, just as it had in the eighth, and bounded into left field. Ruel came home with the winning run and the nation's capital went berserk, President Calvin Coolidge among them.

It was Johnson's finest moment and the Senator's as well, because they never won another World Series. That's simply the way the ball bounced.

The Double No-hit Game

Generally, pitchers have the upper hand in baseball. They (theoretically) know where the ball is going, while the hitter doesn't. Yet every three or four at-bats, a major league hitter will find a way to get a hit. And once a year or so, a pitcher will incredibly not allow a base hit for an entire game. It is a rare enough feat, but on May 2, 1917 it happened twice when Fred Toney and James "Hippo" Vaughn stopped time and the batters of the Cincinnati Reds and Chicago Cubs for nine improbable innings.

Toney, a strapping 6-foot-6, 245-pound right-hander, had come to the Redlegs from the Cubs, where he had been a teammate of Vaughn's in 1913. They won only seven games between them that season—hardly offering any clues that they would make history four years later. Yet as it turned out, 1917 would be the best year ever for the two pitchers. Vaughn, a 6-foot-4, 215-pound left-hander, would win 23 games, one fewer than Toney.

The two pitchers hooked up on that May day and, aided by fortune and their teammates, threw nine innings each of no-hit ball. Toney already had his name in the record book, having pitched a 17-inning no-hitter for Winchester (Kentucky) in his first professional season, but without some saving plays by his outfielders he might have remained a minor figure in history. Vaughn, meanwhile, had struck out 10 Cincinnati batters and not permitted one to roam past first base.

And so, the game entered the tenth inning with Vaughn taking the mound. Cincinnati third baseman Gus Getz went out quietly but then shortstop Larry Kopf, who would complete a ten-year career with an unremarkable batting average of .249, managed to punch a ball through the infield for the game's first hit. Suddenly runners sat on first and third when Cy Williams misplayed Hal Chase's fly to right. And up to the plate stepped Jim Thorpe—yes, *the* Jim Thorpe of football fame—who squibbed a bouncer in the direction of Vaughn. He had no play and Kopf and Thorpe were both safe. Toney took the 1-0 lead into the bottom of the tenth and retired the Reds in order.

It had lasted only 110 minutes, but the double no-hitter thrown by Toney and Vaughn is a permanent part of baseball history, and as such it clearly qualifies as one (two?) of baseball's greatest games.

The odds of one no-hitter are fairly long, and two in one game is inconceivable, right? Wrong. Fred Toney of the Cincinnati Reds and the Chicago Cubs' James Vaughn, above, matched each other in the same game.

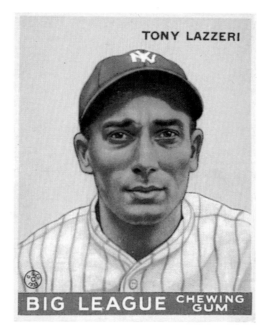

TONY LAZZERI

BIG LEAGUE CHEWING GUM

Alexander Strikes Out Lazzeri

It was a classic confrontation, heightened by the stark contrast of the players involved. In the batter's box at Yankee Stadium stood Tony Lazzeri, a rookie of 23. Thirty-nine-year-old St. Louis Cardinals pitcher Grover Cleveland Alexander, in his 15th major league campaign, scowled at him from the mound. The date was October 9, 1926, and it was the seventh game of the World Series with the Cardinals ahead 3-2 in the seventh inning and the bases loaded.

To that point, the Yankees' young second baseman had distinguished himself by leading the American League with 96 strikeouts. Still, he had knocked in 114 runs for his trouble and was installed as the Yankees' sixth hitter, behind Babe Ruth and Lou Gehrig. Alexander had seen considerably more of the baseball world, with tours of duty in Philadelphia and Chicago. The Cubs procured him from the Athletics in 1917 for two players and $55,000. Alexander, who had averaged 27 wins for seven years in Philadelphia, cooled off in Chicago. On June 22, 1926, the Cardinals picked him up for the modest waiver price and Alexander responded with 9 victories in 16 decisions.

Each player had experienced success in the Series before they squared off in the ultimate game. Alexander struck out 10 batters in the second game and won a 6-2 decision. Lazzeri's sacrifice fly in the tenth inning of the fifth game gave the Yankees a 3-2 Series edge, and Alexander responded with a 10-2 victory in the imperative sixth game.

The Cardinals' one-run lead in the seventh game was in jeopardy when Alexander was called into the game. With the bases loaded, the crowd of 38,093 was screaming. Rogers Hornsby, the St. Louis manager and great Hall of Fame hitter, who had envisioned such a scenario and asked Alexander to limit his celebrating the night before, wanted his ace to pitch to Lazzeri. Alexander needed only three warm-up pitches. A day earlier, Alexander had stopped Lazzeri four times with curve balls, so he threw another one—strike one. Lazzeri drilled an ill-advised fastball down the left field line, foul by only a foot—strike two. Another hard-breaking curve slammed into the glove of catcher Bob O'Farrell, leaving Lazzeri flat-footed, facing Alexander on the mound—strike three.

The rest was anti-climactic. Alexander pitched the last two innings and not many remember that the game ended when Ruth tried to steal second base. Instead, baseball fans remember the day the Cardinals beat the Yankees, and experience conquered youth.

Fred Snodgrass had a servicable bat, as his lifetime batting average of .275 indicates. It is his glove, however, which lives in infamy.

Snodgrass' Big Mistake

Most of baseball's greatest games revolve around heroic feats: Bobby Thomson's monumental home run, Don Larsen's perfect game, Hank Aaron's 755th home run. And there are the unfortunates like New York Giants outfielder Fred Snodgrass, whose name lives in infamy, unless of course you are a Boston Red Sox fan.

Before October 16, 1912, Snodgrass had done little to dishonor himself. In fact, the 5-foot-11, 175-pound center fielder had batted .321 two years earlier and maintained respectable production numbers. Over the regular season in 1912, for instance, Snodgrass scored a career-high 91 runs and knocked in 69 more. He was an adequate outfielder.

The Red Sox and Giants found themselves in the World Series, having obliterated their respective leagues; Boston's 105-47 record was 14 games better than second-place Washington and New York's 103-48 mark bested Pittsburgh by 10. "Smokey" Joe Wood of the Red Sox and the Giants' Rube Marquard had each won two games of the entertaining matchup that stood at three games each. The Series' final game was actually the eighth game between the two teams as the second game had been called on account of darkness with the score tied 6-6 in eleven innings.

After nine exhausting innings in the deciding game, the score was tied at 1-1. The Giants pushed ahead 2-1 in the top of the tenth when Red Murray doubled off Wood and Tris Speaker momentarily juggled Fred Merkle's single to center field. With the great, untiring Christy Mathewson on the mound for New York, the game appeared over. It was at this time that Snodgrass blundered his way into baseball history.

Batting for Wood, Clyde Engle stroked a towering fly toward center. Both Murray and Snodgrass moved for the ball, but Snodgrass called for it. Perhaps he was still thinking about his leadoff out back in the top of the ninth, or maybe Murray's close presence interrupted his concentration. Whatever, the ball hit Snodgrass' glove and then dropped out. Engle arrived safely at second, amazed at his good fortune. Snodgrass atoned partially for the error by robbing the next hitter—Harry Hooper—of an extra-base hit in deep center field. Then Mathewson, still clearly agitated over Snodgrass' blunder, walked Steve Yerkes on four pitches. Like Engle, Speaker was granted a huge favor when the Giants allowed his pop foul to fall harmlessly among three players. He singled on Mathewson's next pitch and delivered Engle home. After Duffy Lewis was walked intentionally, Larry Gardner lofted a long fly to right field and the Red Sox had won the Series. Or, as historians have noted, Snodgrass had lost it.

In 1920, the league-leading Brooklyn Robins (above) battled the relentless Boston Braves in a record-setting 26-inning marathon. The game ended in a 1-1 tie, when it was finally called on account of darkness.

The Longest Game

It was the baseball game that wouldn't end, a 26-inning odyssey that stands today as the longest ever played.

On paper, at least, the May 1, 1920 contest didn't figure. The Brooklyn Robins were on their way to a spectacular 93-61 season and a berth in the World Series. The Boston Braves were destined to finish 30 games back, at 62-90. But for that one day, all things were equal and the two teams finished in a 1-1 tie. No runs were scored in the last twenty innings and, incredibly, both pitchers went the distance. That was their sole gift to history because Joe Oeschger and Leon Cadore each finished modest careers with losing records.

Oeschger, a fastballer, had already distinguished himself the year before by playing for three teams, finishing the season with Boston. Cadore, who threw a curveball, was in his sixth season with the Robins. Oeschger gave in first: catcher Ernie Krueger received one of the pitcher's rare (three) free passes to lead off the fifth, Cadore advanced Krueger to second with a fielder's choice back to Oeschger, and leadoff hitter Ivy Olson knocked in the game's first run with a single to left.

The Braves stormed back in the sixth to tie it when right fielder Walt Cruise reached Cadore for a triple and Tony Boeckel subsequently singled to center. In retrospect, it seems convenient to blame the arm of center fielder Wally Hood for the length of the evening. His throw cut down Boeckel at the plate moments later when he tried to score on a double by shortstop Rabbitt Maranville. And that, quite simply, was that.

It was not without a few scares, though. Brooklyn left fielder Zack Wheat saved a certain extra-base hit with a terrific running catch at the wall. Later, in the 17th inning, the Robins loaded the bases with one out, but Oeschger induced catcher Rowdy Elliot to ground back to the mound and Wheat was forced at the plate. Walter Holke, who tried to score when catcher Hank Gowdy attempted to throw Elliott out at first, was thrown out at home by Brooklyn first baseman Ed Konetchy.

After nearly four hours, umpire Barry McCormick had seen enough—or couldn't see enough, with darkness rapidly moving in. He declared an end to the proceedings one inning short of a total effort equivalent to three regular games. In 1984, the Milwaukee Brewers and Chicago White Sox would play a 25-inning game, but it would only serve to underline the epic nature of that struggle 64 years before.

Harvey Haddix'
Perfect Loss

N o, the world isn't a fair place. Just ask Harvey Haddix, baseball's best example of a man unfairly wronged.

On May 26, 1959, there was no justice for the Pittsburgh Pirates' left-hander. Haddix pitched 12 perfect innings, retired 36 straight batters—and lost to the Milwaukee Braves 1-0 in a thirteen inning game in which the Pirates outhit the Braves 12-1.

The 19,194 fans at Milwaukee's County Stadium could not have been expecting it. At 33, Haddix' best seasons were already behind him. He had won 20 games for St. Louis in 1953, but the Pirates were his fourth team in four years and he was destined to finish the season at a middling 12-12. Lew Burdette was on the mound for Milwaukee, a right-hander. He would be less effective than Haddix, if only from an artistic standpoint.

As Haddix ripped through the Braves' predominantly right-handed lineup with fastballs and sliders, Burdette worked in and out of jams of his own doing. Haddix only flirted with danger twice, and each time shortstop Dick Schofield was fast enough to get Milwaukee shortstop Johnny Logan out. Schofield left his feet to snare Logan's third-inning line drive and in the sixth went deep into the hole between shortstop and third base, came up with the ball, and threw Logan out at first.

The two-out hitter in the ninth, Burdette didn't mind telling Haddix that he was going to break up the no-hit bid. It didn't happen; Burdette missed a two-and-two slider and traditional baseball history-making had been set on its head. Never before had a perfect nine-inning game been thrown without a victory going to the successful pitcher. And as the game progressed the fans backed Haddix more and more with every perfect inning. When he escaped the eleventh, Haddix became the first pitcher to throw a no-hitter of that duration.

Haddix, who stood only 5-foot-9 and weighed 170 pounds, seemed to tire in the twelfth inning. In the unlucky thirteenth, Felix Mantilla became the first Milwaukee baserunner when third baseman Don Hoak took his grounder and threw wildly past first. Eddie Mathews bunted Mantilla to second and slugger Hank Aaron was intentionally passed. The next hitter, first baseman Joe Adcock, had failed to hit the ball out of the infield in four previous at-bats, but he caught a weak slider up in the strike zone and drove it over the fence in right-center for a home run and a 3-0 victory for Milwaukee—or so it seemed. Aaron, however, thought the ball hit at the base of the fence and therefore figured Mantilla had already scored the winning run. He headed toward the Braves' dugout and Adcock ran right past him. Aaron tried to retrace his steps but the next day National League president Warren Giles ruled the official score was 1-0. This was small consolation for Haddix, who, understandably, felt perfectly awful.

Harvey Haddix pitched for St. Louis five seasons, then spent a year each in Philadelphia and Cincinnati before going to the Bucs.

When baseball fans call up memories,
Game Six of the 1975 World Series is
invariably near the top of the list.

1975 World Series, Game Six

There are sometimes games in baseball that transcend the sport itself. On October 21, 1975, the Boston Red Sox and Cincinnati Reds played such a game. Some experts feel it was the greatest game in the greatest World Series in history. Certainly, the 35,205 fans jammed into Fenway Park and the 70 million at home watching on television will never forget it.

It was Cincinnati's Big Red Machine, featuring Pete Rose, Johnny Bench, Joe Morgan, George Foster, and Tony Perez, against the Red Sox, who were trying to recapture the Impossible Dream of 1967 with a cast of characters that included Luis Tiant, Carl Yastrzemski, and Rico Petrocelli. Boston trailed 3-2 in the Series and faced extinction because Perez had ended an 0-15 streak in dramatic fashion by hitting two home runs in the previous game.

After a five-day rain delay, the Red Sox, playing as though their lives depended on it, jumped out to a 3-0 lead in the first inning. Center fielder Fred Lynn hoisted a Gary Nolan pitch into the darkness and the fans in Boston dared to believe in miracles. Tiant, the only Red Sox pitcher to beat the Reds so far, had drawn this critical mound assignment. In the Cincinnati fifth, Tiant looked vulnerable when right fielder Ken Griffey tripled off the wall in center, just over the head of a diving Lynn who also bounced off the wall. That scored Ed Armbrister and Rose, who had reached previously on a walk and a single. Bench's single delivered Griffey with the tying run.

Cincinnati took a 5-3 lead in the seventh inning when Foster doubled and added another run in the eighth on a solo home run by Cesar Geronimo. At that point, El Tiante was asked to leave and it looked like the Boston fans would be disappointed yet again. Yet in the bottom half of the inning pinch-hitter Bernie Carbo stepped to the plate with Lynn and Petrocelli on base. Rawly Eastwick seemed to have Carbo jammed on a three-two fastball, but Carbo got enough to foul the ball off. The next pitch, a pretty fair fastball, landed 400 feet away over the center field fence. Now knotted at 6-6, a great game became greater. And greater with each inning.

Foster nailed Boston second baseman Denny Doyle at the plate in the ninth inning, and in the eleventh Red Sox right fielder Dwight Evans took a home run away from Morgan with a splendid leaping catch and completed a double play by throwing to first. Then, at 12:35 a.m., Boston catcher Carlton Fisk provided the only possible climax to a game of such magnitude. He faced Cincinnati's eighth pitcher, Pat Darcy, and hit his one-ball offering down the left field line. And there was Fisk, all boyish innocence, waving the ball fair with both arms. Mouth open, he watched the wind push the ball back into play, barely, and into the great screen over left field. He jumped for joy and circled the bases with glee.

The Red Sox would lose the seventh game a night later, 4-3, on Morgan's two-out single in the ninth, but something—everything—that had touched Game Six was missing in that contest.

1986 World Series, Game Six

Even the most fatalistic Red Sox fan could allow himself a little room to breathe, a moment at last to ponder the wonder of a World Series championship. Victory would be Boston's this year. In 1967, undermanned Boston had played St. Louis courageously only to lose in the seventh game; in 1975, the Red Sox staged a heroic victory in Game Six before Cincinnati asserted itself and won the Series in the seventh. Now, on October 25th, in the sixth game of the 1986 World Series, Boston pitcher Calvin Schiraldi was a single tenth-inning strike away from ending the New York Mets' season.

Yet, somehow it got away. Again. The Mets, going to a two strike count with three different hitters, put together three singles, then took advantage of a wild pitch by pitcher Bob Stanley and an error by first baseman Bill Buckner to score three runs and win a pulsating 6-5 game at Shea Stadium.

So the Red Sox fulfilled conclusively, it seemed, their role as a team of tragic fate. New York scored all eight of its runs in the last three innings of the seventh game to wrap up the title, 8-5. And the Red Sox were left to wonder how it happened.

Only two weeks earlier, they had been on the other side of agony. The California Angels were themselves a strike away from the World Series when center fielder Dave Henderson hit a home run that eventually carried Boston into extra innings. He drove home the winning run, 7-6, in the eleventh with a sacrifice fly. And so the curse of Angel manager Gene Mauch—that he would never manage in the World Series—was also confirmed.

Henderson had eight hits in the first five games against the Mets, including a triple in the Red Sox 4-2 victory that preceded their ignominious fate in Game Six. He dealt the Mets another blow leading off the tenth inning of that contest with a solo home run. Second baseman Marty Barrett singled home third baseman Wade Boggs to make it 5-3. Schiraldi set down second baseman Wally Backman and first baseman Keith Hernandez on outfield flies. In Hernandez' mind the contest was over, so dejectedly he retired to manager Davey Johnson's office, opened a beer, and watched the game on television. Here is what he saw:

Catcher Gary Carter singled and pinch-hitter Kevin Mitchell hit a two-and-two pitch to follow suit. Ray Knight (who would later be named the Series' Most Valuable Player), faced a two-strike count and also singled. That scored Carter and moved Mitchell to third. Center fielder Mookie Wilson worked the count to two and two, then fouled off two pitches. Mitchell scored when Boston catcher Rich Gedman couldn't stop Stanley's wild pitch to tie the game at 5-5. Then Wilson sent a little bouncer in the direction of Buckner, who lifted his glove prematurely. The ball got behind him and Knight scored the winning run as 55,078 partisans bellowed.

"The ball went skip, skip and it didn't come up," Buckner said later. "The ball missed my glove. I've got to live with it." The same goes for Red Sox fans.

A strike away from elimination, the Mets came back to defeat the Red Sox in heroic fashion. Ray Knight, far left, singled to keep the threat alive in the tenth inning. He later scored the improbable winning run and catcher Gary Carter celebrated with winning pitcher Jesse Orosco.

Three

The Moments

Baseball's ultimate moments are the glittering threads that together form the sport's great tapestry. No athletic pursuit allies itself so readily with myth. Perhaps this is why some of the nation's greatest purveyors of fiction are so consistently attracted to the game. Sometimes it is hard to separate fact from creative fiction.

Did Babe Ruth actually call his gargantuan home run in the third game of the 1932 World Series? Or did the story grow in the telling? Could a pebble in the dust at third base possibly have cost the New York Giants the 1924 World Series? Perhaps. Then there are indisputable moments that need no embellishment. Where were you when Bobby Thomson hit his 'Shot Heard 'Round the World'? People remember. Home runs, and all the sudden grandeur they represent, have created their share of moments. Bill Mazeroski, Hank Aaron, Roger Maris, and Carlton Fisk are legends because their names became identified with singularly dramatic championship-winning home run shots.

Joe DiMaggio was once married to Marilyn Monroe, but that is a footnote in baseball history compared to his 56-game hitting streak. Al Smith and Jim Bagby, Jr., of the Cleveland Indians ended the streak and so became a part of history themselves. Another Indian, the unlikely Bill Wambsganss, made seven put outs in the fifth game of the 1920 World Series against the Brooklyn Robins. What made those outs special was the timing involved. Three of them came in the fifth inning on one play—a ground ball by Clarence Mitchell that Wambsganss turned into the only unassisted triple play the World Series has ever seen.

The 1969 Mets are an example of an entire team which captured a moment. Their ascent from their humble beginnings in 1962 could have come from the pages of a hopelessly romantic novel, although we know it didn't. It is just another moment baseball fans will remember forever.

Where were you when 1) Man landed on the moon, 2) John Kennedy was assassinated, 3) Bobby Thomson hit his historic shot on October 3, 1951? People remember.

Bobby Thomson's "Shot Heard 'Round The World"

Bobby Thomson's 315-foot home run over the left-field wall on October 3, 1951 at the Polo Grounds was easily baseball's most dramatic stroke, a moment frozen in time when all things seemed at once possible. After 157 nail-biting, mind-numbing games, most of them in the wake of the Brooklyn Dodgers, the New York Giants won the pennant, on a single swing of the bat in a battle for the heartstrings of the world's largest city.

It had been a struggle for the Giants to get that far. They had a rookie in center field named Willie Mays but, like the rest of the New York team, he started slowly. On August 12, 1951, the Giants trailed the Dodgers by 13½ games in the National League. Forty-four games later, the teams were locked in a dead heat at 96-58. The Giants won 37 of those final forty-four games, including a string of 16 in a row. Pitchers Sal Maglie and Larry Jansen each won 23 games and New York found itself in a three game playoff series with the Dodgers.

The momentum continued for the Giants as they defeated Brooklyn 3-1 on the strength of home runs by leftfielder Monte Irvin and Thomson, who had been moved by manager Leo Durocher from the outfield to third base the year before. Rookie Clem Labine's six-hitter and a brutal 10-0 Dodger drubbing forced the season to one last confrontation. And so, the championship of the season and the city were reduced to nine innings.

In it, Maglie pitched against Don Newcombe in a battle of 23-game winners. It was tied 1-1 through seven innings, but the Dodgers scored three runs in the eighth. Their last two hits, by Andy Pafko and Billy Cox, appeared to go through Thomson down at third base. There were only three outs left in the 4-1 game when Giant Alvin Dark led off the bottom of the ninth with an infield single. Don Mueller followed with a single himself and there were runners at the corners. Irvin, the clean-up hitter, fouled out and the Giants were a double-play ball away from the end. But Whitey Lockman doubled down the left-field line, which scored Dark and moved Mueller to third, who broke his ankle in his haste. As time was called, Durocher sidled up to Thomson and said with excitement, "If you ever hit one, hit one now."

That brought Thomson, who had been dwelling on his earlier fielding misadventures, back to life. When Durocher saw the Dodgers bring reliever Ralph Branca into the game, he told Thomson to look for a fastball, because Thomson's first-game homer had come off a Branca slider. Sure enough, with a one-strike count Branca delivered the goods. And radio broadcaster Russ Hodges' celebrated call went this way:

"Branca throws…there's a long drive..it's going to be, I believe…The Giants win the pennant! The Giants win the pennant! The Giants win the pennant! The Giants win the pennant!…"

Vic Wertz will never know how Willie Mays caught up to this ball.

Willie Mays' Great Catch

It might have been baseball's greatest catch of all time. That it came at an important time (the eighth inning of a 2-2 contest), in an important game (the first of the 1954 World Series), by an important player (Willie Mays) only made it greater still.

The New York Giants, having held off the Brooklyn Dodgers down the stretch of the season, met the Cleveland Indians, whose record in the American League was 14 games better and itself a record, at 111-43. The Tribe was favored overwhelmingly to handle the Giants, but throughout the Series, Mays simply did not allow defeat. In the first inning of Game 1, Vic Wertz' triple off Sal Maglie gave the Indians a 2-0 lead at the Polo Grounds. Maglie eventually regained his celebrated control and found himself in a 2-2 game after third baseman Hank Thompson singled home two runs in the bottom of the third.

It was still tied when Cleveland centerfielder Larry Doby worked Maglie for a walk to open the eighth inning. Third baseman Al Rosen followed with an infield hit, bringing to the plate Wertz, who had singled twice in addition to his triple. With that in mind, Giants manager Leo Durocher brought in left-hander Don Liddle to pitch. The first pitch was crushed toward deep center field, a 460-foot smash. But Mays, who had been playing customarily shallow, turned and bolted straight for the wall. A few feet away, Mays reached out at full speed, both hands extended, and caught the ball. He turned and threw in one motion, holding Doby at second. Liddle got the next two batters and instead of trailing 4-2, the Giants were still alive.

"Had it all the way," Mays said stepping into the dugout. The same was true of the play he made on Wertz in the tenth inning that was, in many ways, just as scintillating as the eighth-inning catch. Wertz hit a blast to left-center and Mays, running again at full tilt, just managed to stab the ball back-handed and so held Wertz to a double. "It was the toughest chance I had the entire Series," Mays said later, with no apologies to the historians.

With Mays on second base in the bottom of the tenth, by virtue of a walk and stolen base and Hank Thompson standing on first after an intentional walk, "Dusty" Rhodes hit Bob Lemon's hanging curve down the left field line, a scant 258 feet from the plate. That was enough to get it over the fence, however, and the Giants won the Series' first game, 5-2. And though Rhodes was to be the offensive hero in New York's four-game sweep, Mays' glove had allowed it to be.

Note the look of awe on the catcher's face. Note the umpire's smile. Babe Ruth has just crossed the plate after his legendary shot and even teammate Lou Gehrig couldn't believe it.

Babe Ruth's Called Home Run

By Oct. 1, 1932, Babe Ruth's place in history was already secure. He had hit 648 of his astounding 714 home runs, made a lot of money, and produced enough baseball legend and lore to fill several archives. Why then, on this particular autumn day, was the pride of the New York Yankees circling the bases with a grin on his broad face? Why were the fans of the Chicago Cubs rising to their feet at Wrigley Field?

"I just laughed, laughed to myself going around the bases and was thinking what a lucky bum I was," Ruth would say later. For his fifth-inning World Series home run off the Cubs' Charlie Root, a smash to center field that proved to be the longest ball ever hit at Wrigley Field, provided his happiest moment in baseball. More than that, the story would amplify Ruth's greatness as a larger-than-life hero.

It had been a lively Series even before this third game. The invectives had been flowing freely from both dugouts since the Cubbies had voted former Yankee Mark Koenig only a half share of their playoff money after he was brought up from the minors—and since the Yankees took great pains to point out Chicago's penurious ways. Ruth, who never liked to miss any fun, was in the middle of it all.

As Ruth stepped up to the plate in the first inning, Cubs trainer Andy Lotshaw cracked,

"If I had you on my team, I'd hitch you to a wagon," referring to the Bambino's comfortable midsection. Shouts of "Big Belly" and "Balloon Head," followed Ruth to the plate. He promptly took Root to deep center field for a three-run home run.

It was a 4-4 game in the fifth when Ruth called his famous home run. Or didn't. What happened was this: Loosing another barrage of verbiage, the Chicago bench jockeys were rewarded with a disdaining choke sign from Ruth. Then Root quickly threw two called strikes and Ruth raised his index finger, saying, "I still have one left." And the Chicago bench roared. Now, the question of whether Ruth actually pointed to the center field fence or merely waved his finger back at Root, standing sullen on the mound, has never been satisfactorily answered. No matter, Ruth buried the next pitch in the center field seats with a powerful, sweeping swing. It landed roughly where his finger seemed to have pointed and rendered the Cubs silent as Ruth bowed deeply to their dugout as he rounded third. Chicago lost the Series in four straight and the nation gained a delicious piece of history.

"I could have struck out just as well as not because I was mad and I'd made up my mind to swing at the next pitch if I could reach it with a bat," Ruth said later. "When I think of the good breaks in my life—that was one of them."

The Amazin' Mets Of 1969

The 1962 New York Mets were a bad joke. They lost the first nine games in the franchise's history and ultimately finished with a dubious 40-120 record, some 60½ games behind San Francisco in the National League. There was a 17-game losing streak somewhere around Memorial Day and Sandy Koufax blew them away with a no-hitter a month later. Marv Throneberry, who came to New York from the Baltimore Orioles in May, hit .244, his second-best season in the majors, and committed a league-leading 17 errors at first base. Pitcher Roger Craig, bless him, lost 24 games.

Yet for some reason, New Yorkers took to Casey Stengel's bedraggled Mutts. Perhaps it was the radical chic of the times to invest emotionally in a lost cause, or maybe it was just the hot dogs, but 922,530 flocked to the Polo Grounds. The 51-111 Mets finished 48 games out in 1963 and more than a million passed through the doors in New York's last season at the Polo Grounds. The change of venue lifted the Mets to a lofty 53-109 a year later at Shea Stadium. Clearly, these Mets were going somewhere. Just where, no one was quite sure.

This backdrop of futility is necessary to appreciate the Mets' unlikely accomplishment in 1969. They had finished ninth the year before, with a record of 73-89. It would never happen again, because the new concept of divisional play wouldn't allow it. Now, the Mets were part of the National League's East Division—and when the regular season was over they were the best part of it.

Tom Seaver (25-7) captured his first Cy Young Award and nearly threw a perfect game against the Chicago Cubs; the Mets won 11 consecutive games through the straits of Memorial Day; and Cleon Jones carried the New York offense with a .340 batting average. It wasn't easy, however. This was, after all, the Mets. They trailed the Cubs by 9½ games on August 13, then won 38 of 49 to take the East title by eight games. The Atlanta Braves succumbed in three straight playoff games, but not many experts gave the Mets a chance against the Orioles in the World Series.

Baltimore, 109-53 in the American League, had a great pitching staff, featuring Jim Palmer, Dave McNally, and Mike Cuellar, as well as a pair of Hall of Fame Robinsons, Frank and Brooks. When Don Buford hit Seaver's second pitch of the opener for a home run, a lot of people nodded knowingly. The Orioles went on to win that first game, and the series seemed over before it was over. And then something truly amazing happened—the Mets.

They won four straight games. Ed Charles, Jerry Grote, and Al Weis all hit two-out singles in the ninth to win Game Two, 2-1; Tommy Agee and Ron Swoboda made spectacular catches as the Mets prevailed 5-0 and 2-1 in the third and fourth games. They trailed 3-0 in the final game but scored five runs in the last three innings and Shea Stadium erupted. Amazin'!

The greeting at the plate was a fitting welcome for a hero of Bill Mazeroski's magnitude.

Bill Mazeroski's Home Run

That the Pittsburgh Pirates even lasted into the seventh game of the 1960 World Series was accomplishment enough, considering the weight of the evidence against them. Through six games, the New York Yankees had beaten the Bucs by the combined score of 46-17—including nasty victories of 16-3, 10-0, and 12-0—and outhit them 78 to 49. Yet somehow, Pittsburgh had survived to play on that October 13th.

So had Bill Mazeroski, the second baseman from Wheeling, West Virginia. He, like most of the spectators in the stands, knew the Pirates hadn't won a world championship in 35 years. In the sixth inning, it looked like Pittsburgh's chances of going 0-for-36 were quite good. An early 4-0 lead evaporated when the Yankees scored a run in the fifth and four more in the sixth. Catcher Yogi Berra's three-run homer was the big blow. New York made it 7-4 with two more runs in the top of the eighth.

The Pirates scratched their way back into the game, taking advantage of Gino Cimoli's single and Bill Virdon's sharp ground ball that hit shortstop Tony Kubek in the throat. Instead of two outs and no one on, Pittsburgh was in business with men at first and second.

Dick Groat's single scored Cimoli and Bob Skinner moved the runners up. Then, after Rocky Nelson flied to Roger Maris in right, Roberto Clemente reached base on an infield hit that scored Virdon. It was now 7-6. Backup catcher Hal Smith gave Pittsburgh a 9-7 lead when he zeroed in on a Jim Coates offering and drove it out for a three-run homer. The Yankees then tied it in the ninth when Bobby Richardson and pinch-hitter Dale Long led off with singles. Richardson scored on a single by Mickey Mantle and pinch-runner Gil McDougald ran home on Berra's smash down the first base line.

Ralph Terry, New York's big right-hander, would try to force the game into extra innings. For some reason, he threw a high fastball to the leadoff hitter, Mazeroski, a noted crusher of fastballs. The second baseman noted its location and turned on the next pitch, a similar effort pitched slightly lower. Mazeroski was still pumping his arms wildly and bearing down on second base when the roar of the crowd told him the ball had cleared the wall in left-center. He fairly skipped home through the frenzied fans and the Pirates were 10-9 winners. And Mazeroski was the man of a moment that still endures.

You are pitcher Bob Cain and this is your assignment: Throw three pitches to this strike zone that may be a cubic foot in size.

Bill Veeck's Small Experiment

This is the story of Eddie Gaedel and how Bill Veeck, who always had a flair for the bizarre, made him the smallest big-leaguer ever.

Veeck had bought the St. Louis Browns in July, 1951 and immediately set about turning the woeful franchise around. The Browns had finished last or close to it almost every season. The fans disappeared, and Sportsman's Park became a ghost town. So Veeck brought creaking Satchel Paige over from the Cleveland Indians and, because the pitcher was forty-five years old, gave him the best seat in the house—a rocking chair in the bull-pen. There were other flourishes: Marty Marion and Harry Breecheen, who as former Cardinals had marquee value, were added as coaches and the fabulous Dizzy Dean was placed behind the microphone.

Under the guise of a double birthday extravaganza—the American League and the Browns' beer sponsor, Falstaff, were celebrating—Veeck sprung his most (in)famous pro-motional trap. More than 18,000 fans were lured into Sportsman's Park on that August 18th and the Browns, true to form, lost the first game of a doubleheader to the Detroit Tigers. Between games there was a parade of sorts and a cake-cutting ceremony. And out of a seven-foot cake popped Eddie Gaedel, a forty-three-inch, 65-pound midget.

Veeck had booked him through a theatrical agent in Chicago and brought him very quietly to St. Louis where he was dressed in a child's baseball uniform emblazoned with the number ⅛. When Gaedel stepped into the batter's box to lead off for St. Louis in the bottom of the first, umpire Ed Hurley, figuring the halftime show should have been long over, tried to throw him out. But a valid major-league contract was displayed and Gaedel settled in to await Bob Cain's first pitch, waving his toy bat menacingly.

Down in a crouch, Gaedel offered a strike zone of about a square foot, which wasn't nearly big enough for the flustered Cain. Four straight balls sailed in to catcher Bob Swift and Gaedel, who had been instructed by Veeck to resist swinging at anything, pranced to first base. When a pinch-runner was sent in, Gaedel waved his tiny cap to the now delirious crowd. One day later, the baseball purists predictably moved to ban midgets from further play. But the memory of Eddie Gaedel lingers. You can still find him today in the *Baseball Encyclopedia,* tucked in between Len Gabrielson and Gary Gaetti.

There it goes…kiss that baby goodbye.
Roger Maris' 61st homer in the 1961
season produced dramatically
controversial results.

Roger Maris' 61st*
Home Run

The asterisk is gone now, but the scars Roger Maris suffered remain in the memory of all who love baseball. In 1961 he challenged—and conquered—the most hallowed of baseball's single-season records: Babe Ruth's 60-home run mark. And he suffered a lot of grief for his considerable effort.

Maris was a 27-year-old right fielder who had shown a flair for hitting home runs in his first season with the Yankees. He was the American League's Most Valuable Player in 1960, with 39 homers and 112 runs batted in. Maris didn't lead the league that year—Mickey Mantle, in a stout display of one-upmanship, finished the year with 40—but he would in 1961, the first year of the expanded schedule. When Ruth had worn pinstripes in 1927, he set the record in 154 games. Now, the American League would play 162 games.

Maris, a 6-foot, 197-pounder, started slowly. His first home run from the left side of the plate came in the season's eleventh game off Paul Foytack of Detroit. And then Maris got hot; he hit 11 homers in May and added 15 more in June. By July 1st, Maris had hit 28 home runs, compared to Mantle's 27. He was also five games ahead of Ruth's pace. As the season lengthened so did the lines at Maris' locker. Sportswriters wanted to know his feelings as he hunted down "The Bambino." Maris, who had always guarded his privacy zealously,

didn't handle it well. In truth, he had never had good press and the record chase merely exacerbated the situation.

As Maris stroked his way through July, adding 13 more home runs, the baseball establishment grew nervous. Commissioner Ford Frick decreed that Maris would not officially break Ruth's record unless he did it in the same 154 games Ruth had. Thus the potential asterisk was introduced. It haunted Maris to the very end of the season.

He had already tied Ruth on September 26, homering against Baltimore's Jack Fisher and now his last chance would come at Yankee Stadium against Boston on October 1. A crowd of 23,154 watched Maris fly weakly to left off rookie Tracy Stallard in the first inning. In the fourth, Maris stepped in again and drilled Stallard's two-ball pitch 10 rows into the right field stands. The fans understandably went wild. Maris trotted around the bases and, approaching the dugout, found his way blocked. His teammates forced him into four hat-waving encores before they relented.

The debate persists, unfairly, to this day. Should Maris get credit for the record? Certainly he played in 10 more games than Ruth did in his historic season and had 50 more at-bats. Yet, no one has hit 61 home runs before or since Maris—and that speaks for itself.

After the big blast, Aaron had everything—the record, the ball, and a hug from his wife.

Hank Aaron's 715th Home Run

The politicians had already had their say: Hank Aaron was baseball's community property and therefore the Atlanta Braves' left fielder would play the opening series of the 1974 season at Cincinnati. Ordinarily there wouldn't have been such a fuss, but this was history and baseball commissioner Bowie Kuhn insisted it be shared with the rest of the National League.

Aaron had been intently cracking home runs through the years—713 through twenty seasons—leading up to this spring of incredible attention. That, of course, left him one shy of Babe Ruth's career record and when the Braves made noises about saving him for Atlanta Stadium, Kuhn stepped in. Sure enough, Aaron, a graceful 6-foot, 180-pound package from Mobile, Alabama, took his first swing at a Jack Billingham pitch and lost it 400 feet away, far over the left-center field wall at Riverfront Stadium. The nation discussed Aaron's home run number 714 with vigor for four days.

On April 8th, a crowd of 53,775 crammed into Atlanta Stadium hoping this would be the night that Aaron would make them witness to another dramatic milestone in baseball's grand tradition. The bright lights of national television followed his every move, but Aaron refused to blink. He led off the second inning against the Los Angeles Dodgers with a walk. Pitcher Al Downing, whose unhappy lot it was to pitch the game and potentially become the wrong half of a trivia answer, followed a one-and-one count with three straight balls. The crowd was not amused.

Aaron, looking older than his forty years, returned to the plate in the fourth inning with Darrell Evans standing on first. Downing threw another ball, his fourth straight. Then, at 9:07 p.m., Aaron took his first swing of the night. It was the only one he needed. He delivered Downing's fastball over the wall in left field and into the glove of reliever Tom House, who was standing in the Braves' bullpen.

There it was: 715. Yet it fails to convey the enormity of the task achieved. Aaron, who finished his career with 755 home runs, nearly 33 a season for 23 years. How about that?

The End Of Joe DiMaggio's 56-Game Streak

I f taking a round bat and a round ball and trying to hit it square is the most difficult singular feat in sport, then what to make of Joe DiMaggio's 56-game hitting streak from May 15 to July 16, 1941? Call it the greatest sports accomplishment through the ages and you won't be far from wrong.

It began harmlessly enough when the New York Yankees' center fielder singled in four plate appearances against Edgar Smith, a left-hander for the Chicago White Sox. On May 14, DiMaggio had taken the collar, going 0-for-3 against the Cleveland Indians' Mel Harder, who would only pitch 69 innings that year. At the time, New York was idling along at .500 after a disappointing third-place finish in 1940. DiMaggio had led the American League in hitting that year with a .352 average and he would surpass that figure in this magnificent season.

The first milestone DiMaggio passed was Rogers Hornsby's National League record of hitting in 33 consecutive games. In Washington, DiMaggio caught and passed George Sisler, who had held the American League record of 41. The last hurdle was Wee Willie Keeler's nineteenth-century mark of 44 and Boston's Heber Newsome obliged DiMaggio, yielding a homer that ran his streak to 45. The string stood at 56 games when a crowd of 67,468 turned out at Cleveland's Municipal Stadium on July 17th.

The Indians had been the last team to shut DiMaggio down and left-handed starter Al Smith seemed to be continuing the trend with some help from Ken Keltner at the hot corner. Keltner turned two DiMaggio smashes down the third-base line into outs with terrific back-handed stops. Smith had walked DiMaggio the second time he batted. DiMaggio's fourth and last chance came against Jim Bagby, a right-hander who would finish his career with a 97-96 record. The bases were loaded and there was one out in the eighth when DiMaggio lashed a shot to shortstop. Lou Boudreau, seeing the ball take a bad bounce, grabbed it with his bare hand and shoveled it to second baseman Ray Mack, who relayed it to first for a double-play.

DiMaggio would go on to hit the next 16 straight games and finish the season with a batting average of .357. And the Yankees would ride into first place along with him. During DiMaggio's 56-game streak, New York won 41 games and went on to clinch an early pennant and take a five game World Series from the Brooklyn Dodgers. The record still stands today and may last as long as baseball itself.

A fiercely determined Joe DiMaggio set baseball's most unassailable record.

Bill Wambsganss'
Unassisted Triple Play

Timing, they say, is everything. Consider the very special case of William Adolph Wambsganss, who placed himself as the right man in the right place at the right time to make some overwhelming World Series history on October 10, 1920.

Wambsganss was never known as an extraordinary player during his 13 years in the American League. The second baseman's career batting average was .259 and his fielding usually proved adequate. This was to be his one and only Series and Wambsganss would make it count. The stage was set as the Brooklyn Robins and Wambsganss' Cleveland Indians, tied at two games each, headed into Game Five at League Park.

In the first inning Indians' outfielder Elmer Smith hit the first grand slam in World Series history. It was still 4-0 in the fourth when Jim Bagby made his bid for the record books and took a Burleigh Grimes spitball into the center field bleachers. It was the first Series home run by a pitcher and gave Bagby a comfortable working margin of 7-0. And no one would ever remember this game if Wambsganss hadn't forced himself into the scenario.

Pete Kilduff, the second baseman, led off the Brooklyn fifth with a single and moved to second on catcher Otto Miller's single. And up came the pitcher, Clarence Mitchell. As hurlers go, Mitchell wasn't a bad hitter at all. The season before he had produced 18 hits in 49 at-bats for a robust .367 average. Realizing that Mitchell was a dangerous left-handed pull hitter, Wambsganss crept back on the grass. When Mitchell hit a Bagby fastball on a line up the middle, Wambsganss threw himself at the ball—and caught it. Kilduff, assuming the ball was headed for center field, was nearly into third when Wambsganss stepped on second to double him up. Turning quickly toward first, the second baseman spotted Miller standing just a few feet away, frozen in his tracks. Wambsganss made two short steps to his left and tagged Miller on the shoulder. One, two, three. Wambsganss had turned the only unassisted triple play in World Series history.

1876 • The National League is formed on February 2.

1880 • The Cincinnati franchise is thrown out of the league for serving liquor in the stands and playing on Sunday.

1909 • National League President Harry C. Pulliam has a nervous breakdown and kills himself with a pistol on July 29.

1912 • Ty Cobb is suspended on May 15 for jumping into the grandstands and fighting a fan. His teammates refuse to play until the suspension is lifted, forcing the Detroit front office to gather an impromtu team to play the Philadelphia Athletics. The one-day major leaguers lose, 23-2. Cobb is reinstated on May 26.

1920 • Cleveland's Ray Chapman is hit by Yankee pitcher Carl May's fastball, and dies the next day, thus becoming the first and only fatality of major league baseball.

1925 • Babe Ruth is fined a record $5,000 for insubordination and breaking club training rules.

1941 • Joe DiMaggio hits safely in 56 consecutive games.

1945 • The St. Louis Browns sign Pete Gray, a one-armed outfielder.

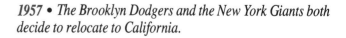

1949 • Philadelphia Philly Eddie Waitkus is shot in the lung by a deranged fan who lured him to her hotel room in Chicago. "If I couldn't have him, neither could anybody else," she later says. Waitkus recovers and continues to play.

1953 • On May 6, the St. Louis Browns' "Bobo" Holloman becomes the first pitcher to throw a no-hitter in his debut in the majors. By July 23, the 3-7 Bobo is sent back to the minor leagues, never to play in the majors again.

1956 • Don Larsen pitches the first no-hitter in a World Series.

1957 • The Brooklyn Dodgers and the New York Giants both decide to relocate to California.

1901 • *The American League is formed.*

1903 • *16,242 witness the first World Series game on October 1, between the Boston Red Sox and Pittsburgh Pirates. The Pirates win, 7-3, but drop the series in seven games.*

1916 • *For the first time in ten years, Ty Cobb (.371) loses the American League batting title; Tris Speaker (.386) ends his unprecedented dominance.*

1919 • *The Chicago White Sox throw the World Series to the Cincinnati Reds. Scandal erupts. Within a year, eight White Sox players are barred from the major leagues forever.*

1936 • *The Baseball Hall of Fame in Cooperstown, New York is founded. Ty Cobb is its first inductee.*

1947 • *Jackie Robinson becomes the first black player in the major leagues.*

1951 • *Topps introduces the first baseball card. It is packed with caramel candy instead of gum.*

1955 • *Cy Young and Honus Wagner die within a month of each other.*

1958 • *Dodger Roy Campanella is paralyzed in a Long Island auto accident, ending his career.*

1959 • *Hank Aaron, home run king, led the National League with a batting average of .355, and still managed to hit 39 home runs.*

1961 • *Roger Maris hits 61 home runs, in a 162-game season (which is eight games more than the traditional 154-game season), breaking Babe Ruth's record amid controversy. Maris enters the record books with an asterisk as a result.*

1964 • *The Boyer family is divided about the World Series: Ken Boyer plays third base for the St. Louis Cards; brother Clete is at third for the opposing Yankees.*

1966 • *Artificial turf is introduced to baseball. Philly Dick Allen sums up the purists' opinion with, "I don't want to play on any grass a cow wouldn't eat."*

1967 • *Denny McClain injures two toes chasing racoons, he says, and is sidelined. Later,* Sports Illustrated *contends that McClain's injury were caused by a mob leader in response to gambling debts. Three years later Bowie Kuhn suspends him for "bookmaking activities in 1967 and associations at the time."*

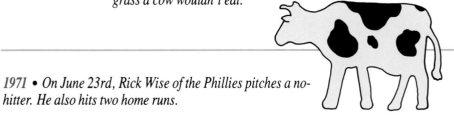

1971 • *On June 23rd, Rick Wise of the Phillies pitches a no-hitter. He also hits two home runs.*

1972 • *The first player strike in baseball history begins on April 1st, ending 13 days later.*

1974 • *The Cleveland Indians declare their June 4 contest against the Texas Indians "Beer Night," during which fans can get a cup of beer for just 10 cents. Fights break out in the stands, firecrackers are thrown in the Rangers' dugout, and in the ninth inning, fans storm the field. The Indians forfeit the game.*

Disco Madness

Disco Madness

1977 • *Players' salaries jump 45 percent in one year. The Yankees raise their upper grandstand admission price from $1.50 to $4.50.*

1979 • *The June 12 Chicago-Detroit doubleheader is labeled Disco Demolition Night, in which fans bringing a disco record to be burned between games are admitted for 98 cents. Between games bases are torn up, fires are set, and 37 fans arrested. Chicago forfeits the second game.*

1983 • *On July 24 George Brett hits a two-run homer in the ninth inning against the Yankees, but it is found that pine tar, on the bat for a better grip, was higher than the rulebook allowed. The runs are nullified. Kansas City protests, the runs reinstated, and a date set for the play to resume. Tempers flare, and George Steinbrenner is fined $250,000 by Bowie Kuhn for "certain public statements" regarding the incident.*

1983 • *Yankee center fielder Dave Winfield accidently throws a ball at a sea gull during a game with Toronto, killing the bird. Winfield is arrested by Toronto police, and fined $500 for . "willfully causing unnecessary cruelty to animals." The charges are eventually dropped.*

1965 • *The free agent draft becomes a reality. Nineteen-year-old Arizona State University outfielder Rick Monday is reportedly paid $100,000 to sign with the Kansas City Athletics.*

1969 • *The All-Star game is rained out for the first time.*

1970 • *While on the witness stand in a case brought by Curt Flood of the Phillies which challenged baseball's Reserve Clause, player-turned broadcaster Joe Garagiola tells the judge, "I wish you were on a baseball card. I'd have you."*

1973 • *The designated hitter is introduced.*

1973 • *George Steinbrenner buys the Yankees, saying "I look forward to coming to town just to see the games...We plan absentee ownership."*

1975 • *0-2 pitcher Burt Hooton is traded from the Cubs to the Dodgers. He winds up with 18 victories.*

1976 • *Twenty-two-year-old Detroit pitcher Mark Fidrych emerges as the year's phenomenon. He talks to the ball before throwing, flaps his arms on the mound (thus earning the nickname "Big Bird"), and ends the season with a 19-9 record, leading the league in complete games and ERA.*

1978 • *Dodger pitcher Don Sutton, long suspected of doctoring the ball, gets the last laugh when an umpire checks Sutton's glove for foreign substances and instead found a note which reads, "You're getting warm, but it's still not here."*

1981 • *The Major League Players Association strikes for 50 days in the summer. The cost? Fans are openly hostile, 713 games are missed, and an estimated $98 million in revenue is lost.*

1982 • *The Atlanta Braves win their first 13 games of the season, a record. Later, they remove a teepee of their mascot, Chief Noc-A-Homa, from the left field stands, and quickly drop 15 of the next 16 games. The teepee then returns.*

1985 • *Former Philadelphia Phillies' clubhouse caterer Curtis Strong is convicted of selling cocaine to a variety of baseball players.*

1987 • *A cheating epidemic resurfaces. Pitcher Joe Niekro is suspended for carrying an emery board in his back pocket; various players are accused of corking their bats. Commissioner Peter Ueberroth decrees that teams will be permitted to impound one bat belonging to an opponent per game.*

Year	Winner	Won	Lost	Pct
1901	Pittsburgh	90	49	.647
1902	Pittsburgh	103	36	.741
1903	Pittsburgh	91	49	.650
1904	New York	106	47	.693
1905	New York	105	48	.686
1906	Chicago	116	36	.763
1907	Chicago	107	45	.704
1908	Chicago	99	55	.643
1909	Pittsburgh	110	42	.724
1910	Chicago	104	50	.675
1911	New York	99	54	.647
1912	New York	103	48	.682
1913	New York	101	51	.664
1914	Boston	94	59	.614
1915	Philadelphia	90	62	.592
1916	Brooklyn	94	60	.610
1917	New York	98	56	.636
1918	Chicago	84	45	.651
1919	Cincinnati	96	44	.686
1920	Brooklyn	93	60	.604
1921	New York	94	56	.614
1922	New York	93	61	.604
1923	New York	95	58	.621
1924	New York	93	60	.608
1925	Pittsburgh	95	58	.621
1926	St. Louis	89	65	.578
1927	Pittsburgh	94	60	.610
1928	St. Louis	95	59	.617
1929	Chicago	98	54	.645
1930	St. Louis	92	62	.597
1931	St. Louis	101	53	.656
1932	Chicago	90	64	.584
1933	New York	91	61	.599
1934	St. Louis	95	58	.621
1935	Chicago	100	54	.649
1936	New York	91	62	.597
1937	New York	95	57	.625
1938	Chicago	89	63	.586
1939	Cincinnati	97	57	.630
1940	Cincinnati	100	53	.654
1941	Brooklyn	100	54	.649
1942	St. Louis	106	48	.688
1943	St. Louis	105	49	.682
1944	St. Louis	105	49	.682
1945	Chicago	98	56	.636
1946	St. Louis	98	58	.628
1947	Brooklyn	94	60	.610
1948	Boston	91	62	.595
1949	Brooklyn	97	57	.630
1950	Philadelphia	91	63	.591
1951	New York	98	59	.624
1952	Brooklyn	96	57	.627
1953	Brooklyn	105	49	.682
1954	New York	97	57	.630
1955	Brooklyn	98	55	.641
1956	Brooklyn	93	61	.604
1957	Milwaukee	95	59	.617
1958	Milwaukee	92	62	.597
1959	Los Angeles	88	68	.564
1960	Pittsburgh	95	59	.617
1961	Cincinnati	93	61	.604
1962	San Francisco	103	62	.624
1963	Los Angeles	99	63	.611
1964	St. Louis	93	69	.574
1965	Los Angeles	97	65	.599
1966	Los Angeles	95	67	.586
1967	St. Louis	101	60	.627
1968	St. Louis	97	65	.599

Year	East Winner	W	L	Pct	West Winner	W	L	Pct	Playoff Winner
1969	N.Y. Mets	100	62	.617	Atlanta	93	69	.574	N.Y. Mets
1970	Pittsburgh	89	73	.549	Cincinnati	102	60	.630	Cincinnati
1971	Pittsburgh	97	65	.599	San Francisco	90	72	.556	Pittsburgh
1972	Pittsburgh	96	59	.619	Cincinnati	95	59	.617	Cincinnati
1973	N.Y. Mets	82	79	.509	Cincinnati	99	63	.611	N.Y. Mets
1974	Pittsburgh	88	74	.543	Los Angeles	102	60	.630	Los Angeles
1975	Pittsburgh	92	69	.571	Cincinnati	108	54	.667	Cincinnati
1976	Philadelphia	101	61	.623	Cincinnati	102	60	.630	Cincinnati
1977	Philadelphia	101	61	.623	Los Angeles	98	64	.605	Los Angeles
1978	Philadelphia	90	72	.556	Los Angeles	95	67	.586	Los Angeles
1979	Pittsburgh	98	64	.605	Cincinnati	90	71	.559	Pittsburgh
1980	Philadelphia	91	71	.562	Houston	93	70	.571	Philadelphia
1981	Philadelphia	34	21	.618	Los Angeles	36	21	.632	Los Angeles
1981	Montreal	30	23	.566	Houston	33	20	.623	Montreal
1982	St. Louis	92	70	.588	Atlanta	89	73	.549	St. Louis
1983	Philadelphia	90	72	.556	Los Angeles	91	71	.562	Philadelphia
1984	Chicago	96	65	.596	San Diego	92	70	.568	San Diego
1985	St. Louis	101	61	.623	Los Angeles	95	67	.586	St. Louis
1986	N.Y. Mets	108	54	.667	Houston	96	66	.593	N.Y. Mets
1987	St. Louis	95	67	.586	San Francisco	90	72	.556	St. Louis
1988	N.Y. Mets	100	60	.625	Los Angeles	94	67	.584	Los Angeles

Year	Winner	Won	Lost	Pct
1901	Chicago	83	53	.610
1902	Philadelphia .	83	53	.610
1903	Boston......	91	47	.659
1904	Boston......	95	59	.617
1905	Philadelphia .	92	56	.622
1906	Chicago	93	58	.616
1907	Detroit......	92	58	.613
1908	Detroit......	90	63	.588
1909	Detroit......	98	54	.645
1910	Philadelphia .	102	48	.680
1911	Philadelphia .	101	50	.669
1912	Boston......	105	47	.691
1913	Philadelphia .	96	57	.627
1914	Philadelphia .	99	53	.651
1915	Boston......	101	50	.669
1916	Boston......	91	63	.591
1917	Chicago	100	54	.649
1918	Boston......	75	51	.595
1919	Chicago	88	52	.629
1920	Cleveland ...	98	56	.636
1921	New York ...	98	55	.641
1922	New York ...	94	60	.610
1923	New York ...	98	54	.645
1924	Washington..	92	62	.597
1925	Washington..	96	55	.636
1926	New York ...	91	63	.591
1927	New York ...	110	44	.714
1928	New York ...	101	53	.656
1929	Philadelphia .	104	46	.693
1930	Philadelphia .	102	52	.662
1931	Philadelphia .	107	45	.704
1932	New York ...	107	47	.695
1933	Washington..	99	53	.651
1934	Detroit......	101	53	.656
1935	Detroit......	93	58	.616
1936	New York ...	102	51	.667
1937	New York ...	102	52	.662
1938	New York ...	99	53	.651
1939	New York ...	106	45	.702
1940	Detroit......	90	64	.584
1941	New York ...	101	53	.656
1942	New York ...	103	51	.669
1943	New York ...	98	56	.636
1944	St. Louis	89	65	.578
1945	Detroit......	88	65	.575
1946	Boston......	104	50	.675
1947	New York ...	97	57	.630
1948	Cleveland ...	97	58	.626
1949	New York ...	97	57	.630
1950	New York ...	98	56	.636
1951	New York ...	98	56	.636
1952	New York ...	95	59	.617
1953	New York ...	99	52	.656
1954	Cleveland ...	111	43	.721
1955	New York ...	96	58	.623
1956	New York ...	97	57	.630
1957	New York ...	98	56	.636
1958	New York ...	92	62	.597
1959	Chicago	94	60	.610
1960	New York ...	97	57	.630
1961	New York ...	109	53	.673
1962	New York ...	96	66	.593
1963	New York ...	104	57	.646
1964	New York ...	99	63	.611
1965	Minnesota ...	102	60	.630
1966	Baltimore....	97	63	.606
1967	Boston......	92	70	.568
1968	Detroit......	103	59	.636

PENNANT WINNERS–American League

	East				West				Playoff
Year	Winner	W	L	Pct	Winner	W	L	Pct	Winner
1969	Baltimore...	109	53	.673	Minnesota ..	97	65	.599	Baltimore
1970	Baltimore...	108	54	.667	Minnesota ..	98	64	.605	Baltimore
1971	Baltimore...	101	57	.639	Oakland ...	101	60	.627	Baltimore
1972	Detroit.....	86	70	.551	Oakland ...	93	62	.600	Oakland
1973	Baltimore...	97	65	.599	Oakland ...	94	68	.580	Oakland
1974	Baltimore...	91	71	.562	Oakland ...	90	72	.556	Oakland
1975	Boston.....	95	65	.594	Oakland ...	98	64	.605	Boston
1976	N.Y.Yankees	97	62	.610	Kansas City .	90	72	.556	N.Y.Yankees
1977	N.Y.Yankees	100	62	.617	Kansas City .	102	60	.630	N.Y.Yankees
1978	N.Y.Yankees	100	63	.613	Kansas City .	92	70	.568	N.Y.Yankees
1979	Baltimore...	102	57	.642	California ..	88	74	.543	Baltimore
1980	N.Y.Yankees	103	59	.636	Kansas City .	97	65	.599	Kansas City
1981	N.Y.Yankees	34	22	.607	Oakland ...	37	23	.617	N.Y.Yankees
1981	Milwaukee	31	22	.585	Kansas City .	30	23	.566	Kansas City
1982	Milwaukee	95	67	.586	California ..	93	69	.574	Milwaukee
1983	Baltimore...	98	64	.605	Chicago.....	99	63	.611	Baltimore
1984	Detroit.....	104	58	.642	Kansas City .	84	78	.519	Detroit
1985	Toronto	99	62	.615	Kansas City .	91	71	.562	Kansas City
1986	Boston.....	95	66	.590	California ..	92	70	.568	Boston
1987	Detroit.....	98	64	.605	Minnesota ..	85	77	.525	Minnesota
1988	Boston.....	89	73	.549	Oakland ...	104	58	.642	Oakland

*Due to the 1981 players' strike, there were four divisional winners (instead of two), and two pennant winners (instead of one) in each league.

WORLD SERIES RESULTS

Year	Result	Year	Result
1903	Boston AL 5, Pittsburgh NL 3	1946	St. Louis NL 4, Boston AL 3
1904	No series	1947	New York AL 4, Brooklyn NL 3
1905	New York NL 4, Philadelphia AL 1	1948	Cleveland AL 4, Boston NL 2
1906	Chicago AL 4, Chicago NL 2	1949	New York AL 4, Brooklyn NL 1
1907	Chicago NL 4, Detroit AL 0, 1 tie	1950	New York AL 4, Philadelphia NL 0
1908	Chicago NL 4, Detroit AL 1	1951	New York AL 4, New York NL 2
1909	Pittsburgh NL 4, Detroit AL 3	1952	New York AL 4, Brooklyn NL 3
1910	Philadelphia AL 4, Chicago NL 1	1953	New York AL 4, Brooklyn NL 2
1911	Philadelphia AL 4, New York NL 2	1954	New York NL 4, Cleveland AL 0
1912	Boston AL 4, New York NL 3, 1 tie	1955	Brooklyn NL 4, New York AL 3
1913	Philadelphia AL 4, New York NL 1	1956	New York AL 4, Brooklyn NL 3
1914	Boston NL 4, Philadelphia AL 0	1957	Milwaukee NL 4, New York AL 3
1915	Boston AL 4, Philadelphia NL 1	1958	New York AL 4, Milwaukee NL 3
1916	Boston AL 4, Brooklyn NL 1	1959	Los Angeles NL 4, Chicago AL 2
1917	Chicago AL 4, New York NL 2	1960	Pittsburgh NL 4, New York AL 3
1918	Boston AL 4, Chicago NL 2	1961	New York AL 4, Cincinnati NL 1
1919	Cincinnati NL 5, Chicago AL 3	1962	New York AL 4, San Francisco NL 3
1920	Cleveland AL 5, Brooklyn NL 2	1963	Los Angeles NL 4, New York AL 0
1921	New York NL 5, New York AL 3	1964	St. Louis NL 4, New York AL 3
1922	New York NL 4, New York AL 0, 1 tie	1965	Los Angeles NL 4, Minnesota AL 3
1923	New York AL 4, New York NL 2	1966	Baltimore AL 4, Los Angeles NL 0
1924	Washington AL 4, New York NL 3	1967	St. Louis NL 4, Boston AL 3
1925	Pittsburgh NL 4, Washington AL 3	1968	Detroit AL 4, St. Louis NL 3
1926	St. Louis NL 4, New York AL 3	1969	New York NL 4, Baltimore AL 1
1927	New York AL 4, Pittsburgh NL 0	1970	Baltimore AL 4, Cincinnati NL 1
1928	New York AL 4, St. Louis NL 0	1971	Pittsburgh NL 4, Baltimore AL 3
1929	Philadelphia AL 4, Chicago NL 1	1972	Oakland AL 4, Cincinnati NL 3
1930	Philadelphia AL 4, St. Louis NL 2	1973	Oakland AL 4, New York NL 3
1931	St. Louis NL 4, Phildelphia AL 3	1974	Oakland AL 4, Los Angeles NL 1
1932	New York AL 4, Chicago NL 0	1975	Cincinnati NL 4, Boston AL 3
1933	New York NL 4, Washington AL 1	1976	Cincinnati NL 4, New York AL 0
1934	St. Louis NL 4, Detroit AL 3	1977	New York AL 4, Los Angeles NL 2
1935	Detroit AL 4, Chicago NL 2	1978	New York AL 4, Los Angeles NL 2
1936	New York AL 4, New York NL 2	1979	Pittsburgh NL 4, Baltimore AL 3
1937	New York AL 4, New York NL 1	1980	Philadelphia NL 4, Kansas City AL 2
1938	New York AL 4, Chicago NL 0	1981	Los Angeles NL 4, New York AL 2
1939	New York AL 4, Cincinnati NL 0	1982	St. Louis NL 4, Milwaukee AL 3
1940	Cincinnati NL 4, Detroit AL 3	1983	Baltimore AL 4, Philadelphia NL 1
1941	New York AL 4, St. Louis NL 1	1984	Detroit AL 4, San Diego NL 1
1942	St. Louis NL 4, New York AL 1	1985	Kansas City AL 4, St. Louis NL 3
1943	New York AL 4, St. Louis NL 1	1986	New York NL 4, Boston AL 3
1944	St. Louis NL 4, St. Louis AL 2	1987	Minnesota AL 4, St. Louis NL 3
1945	Detroit AL 4, Chicago NL 3	1988	Los Angeles NL 4, Oakland AL 1

HALL OF FAME MEMBERS

The first number in parenthesis indicates the total number of votes possible in a given year. The numbers in parenthesis next to a player's name indicates the amount of votes received. (To be inducted, a player must receive at least 75 percent of the total possible votes.) Members with no corresponding numbers have been inducted by special committee. An asterisk (*) indicates a member who was selected as a non-player.

1936 Total votes (226)
Ty Cobb (222)
Honus Wagner (215)
Babe Ruth (215)
Christy Mathewson (205)
Walter Johnson (189)

1937 Total votes (201)
Nap Lajoie (168)
Tris Speaker (165)
Cy Young (153)
*Morgan B. Bulkeley
*Ban Johnson
Connie Mack
John McGraw
George Wright

1938 Total votes (262)
Pete Alexander (212)
*Alexander Cartwright
*Henry Chadwick

1939 Total votes (274)
George Sisler (235)
Eddie Collins (213)
Willie Keeler (207)
Lou Gehrig (by special election)
Cap Anson
Charlie Comiskey
Candy Cummings
Buck Ewing
Hoss Radbourne
Al Spalding

1942
Rogers Hornsby (182)

1944
*Judge Kenesaw M. Landis

1945
Roger Bresnahan
Dan Brouthers
Fred Clarke
Jimmie Collins
Ed Delahanty
Hugh Duffy
Hughie Jennings
Mike Kelly
Jim O'Rourke
Wilbert Robinson

1946
Jesse Burkett
Frank Chance
Jack Chesbro
Johnny Evers
Clark Griffith
Tom McCarthy
Joe McGinnity
Eddie Plank
Joe Tinker
Rube Waddell
Ed Walsh

1947 Total votes (161)
Carl Hubbell (140)
Frank Frisch (136)
Mickey Cochrane (128)
Lefty Grove (123)

1948 Total votes (121)
Herb Pennock (94)
Pie Traynor (93)

1949 Total votes (187)
Charlie Gehringer (159)
Three-Finger Brown
Kid Nichols

1951 Total votes (226)
Mel Ott (197)
Jimmie Foxx (179)

1952 Total votes (234)
Harry Heilmann (203)
Paul Waner (195)

1953 Total votes (264)
Dizzy Dean (209)
Al Simmons (199)
*Ed Barrow
Chief Bender
*Tom Connolly
*Bill Klem
Bobby Wallace
*Harry Wright

1954 Total votes (252)
Rabbit Maranville (209)
Bill Dickey (202)
Bill Terry (195)

1955 Total votes (251)
Joe DiMaggio (223)
Ted Lyons (217)
Dazzy Vance (205)
Gabby Hartnett (195)
Frank Baker
Ray Schalk

1956 Total votes (193)
Hank Greenberg (164)
Joe Cronin (152)

1957
Sam Crawford
*Joe McCarthy

1959
Zack Wheat

1961
Max Carey
Billy Hamilton

1962 Total votes (160)
Bob Feller (150)
Jackie Robinson (124)
*Bill McKechnie
Edd Roush

1963
John Clarkson
Elmer Flick
Sam Rice
Eppa Rixey

1964 Total votes (225)
Luke Appling (189)
Red Faber
Burleigh Grimes
*Miller Huggins
Tim Keefe
Heinie Manush
John Ward

1965
Pud Galvin

1966 Total votes (302)
Ted Williams (282)
*Casey Stengel

1967 Total votes (306)
Red Ruffing (266)
*Branch Rickey
Lloyd Waner

1968 Total votes (283)
Joe Medwick (240)
Kiki Cuyler
Goose Goslin

1969 Total votes (340)
Stan Musial (317)
Roy Campanella (270)
Stan Coveleski
Waite Hoyt

1970 Total votes (300)
Lou Boudreau (232)
Earle Combs
*Ford Frick
Jesse Haines

1971
Jake Beckley
Dave Bancroft
Chick Hafey
Harry Hooper
Joe Kelley
Rube Marquard
*George Weiss
Satchel Paige

1972 Total votes (396)
Sandy Koufax (344)
Yogi Berra (339)
Early Wynn (301)
Lefty Gomez
*Will Harridge
Ross Youngs
Josh Gibson
Buck Leonard

1973 Total votes (380)
Warren Spahn (316)
*Billy Evans
George Kelly
Mickey Welch
Monte Irvin
Special waiver of
5-year waiting period:
Roberto Clemente

1974 Total votes (365)
Mickey Mantle (322)
Whitey Ford (284)
Jim Bottomley
*Jocko Conlan
Sam Thompson
Cool Papa Bell

1975 Total votes (362)
Ralph Kiner (273)
Earl Averill
*Buckey Harris
Billy Herman
Judy Johnson

1976 Total votes (388)
Robin Roberts (337)
Bob Lemon (305)
Roger Connor
Fred Lindstrom
*Cal Hubbard
Oscar Charleston

1977 Total votes (383)
Ernie Banks (321)
Amos Rusie
Joe Sewell
*Al Lopez
Martin Dihigo
John Henry Lloyd

1978 Total votes (379)
Eddie Mathews (310)
Addie Joss
*Larry MacPhail

1979 Total votes (432)
Willie Mays (409)
*Warren Giles
Hack Wilson

1980 Total votes (385)
Al Kaline (340)
Duke Snider (333)
Chuck Klein
*Tom Yawkey

1981 Total votes (401)
Bob Gibson (337)
Johnny Mize
Rube Foster

1982 Total votes (415)
Hank Aaron (406)
Frank Robinson (370)
Travis Jackson
*Happy Chandler

1983 Total votes (374)
Brooks Robinson (344)
Juan Marichal (313)
George Kell
*Walt Alston

1984 Total votes (403)
Luis Aparicio (341)
Harmon Killebrew (335)
Don Drysdale (316)
Rick Ferrell
Pee Wee Reese

1985 Total votes (395)
Hoyt Wilhelm (331)
Lou Brock (315)

1986 Total votes (425)
Willie McCovey (346)
Bobby Doerr
Ernie Lombardi

1987 Total votes (413)
Billy Williams (354)
Catfish Hunter (315)
Ray Dandridge

MOST VALUABLE PLAYER AWARD WINNERS

as voted by the Baseball Writers' Association

National League	American League
1931 Frank Frisch, St. Louis	1931 Lefty Grove, Philadelphia
1932 Charles Klein, Philadelphia	1932 Jimmy Foxx, Philadelphia
1933 Carl Hubbell, New York	1933 Jimmy Foxx, Philadelphia
1934 Dizzy Dean, St. Louis	1934 Mickey Cochrane, Detroit
1935 Gabby Hartnett, Chicago	1935 Henry Greenberg, Detroit
1936 Carl Hubbell, New York	1936 Lou Gehrig, New York
1937 Joe Medwick, St. Louis	1937 Charley Gehringer, Detroit
1938 Ernie Lombardi, Cincinnati	1938 Jimmy Foxx, Boston
1939 Bucky Walters, Cincinnati	1939 Joe DiMaggio, New York
1940 Frank McCormick, Cincinnati	1940 Hank Greenberg, Detroit
1941 Dolph Camilli, Brooklyn	1941 Joe DiMaggio, New York
1942 Mort Cooper, St. Louis	1942 Joe Gordon, New York
1943 Stan Musial, St. Louis	1943 Spurgeon Chandler, New York
1944 Martin Marion, St. Louis	1944 Hal Newhouser, Detroit
1945 Phil Cavarretta, Chicago	1945 Hal Newhouser, Detroit
1946 Stan Musial, St. Louis	1946 Ted Williams, Boston
1947 Bob Elliott, Boston	1947 Joe DiMaggio, New York
1948 Stan Musial, St. Louis	1948 Lou Boudreau, Cleveland
1949 Jackie Robinson, Brooklyn	1949 Ted Williams, Boston
1950 Jim Konstanty, Philadelphia	1950 Phil Rizzuto, New York
1951 Roy Campanella, Brooklyn	1951 Yogi Berra, New York
1952 Hank Sauer, Chicago	1952 Bobby Shantz, Philadelphia
1953 Roy Campanella, Brooklyn	1953 Al Rosen, Cleveland
1954 Willie Mays, New York	1954 Yogi Berra, New York
1955 Roy Campanella, Brooklyn	1955 Yogi Berra, New York
1956 Don Newcombe, Brooklyn	1956 Mickey Mantle, New York
1957 Henry Aaron, Milwaukee	1957 Mickey Mantle, New York
1958 Ernie Banks, Chicago	1958 Jackie Jensen, Boston
1959 Ernie Banks, Chicago	1959 Nellie Fox, Chicago
1960 Dick Groat, Pittsburgh	1960 Roger Maris, New York
1961 Frank Robinson, Cincinnati	1961 Roger Maris, New York
1962 Maury Wills, Los Angeles	1962 Mickey Mantle, New York
1963 Sandy Koufax, Los Angeles	1963 Elston Howard, New York
1964 Ken Boyer, St. Louis	1964 Brooks Robinson, Baltimore
1965 Willie Mays, San Francisco	1965 Zoila Versailles, Minnesota
1966 Roberto Clemente, Pittsburgh	1966 Frank Robinson, Baltimore
1967 Orlando Cepeda, St. Louis	1967 Carl Yastrzemski, Boston
1968 Bob Gibson, St. Louis	1968 Denny McLain, Detroit
1969 Willie McCovey, San Francisco	1969 Harmon Killebrew, Minnesota
1970 Johnny Bench, Cincinnati	1970 John (Boog) Powell, Baltimore
1971 Joe Torre, St. Louis	1971 Vida Blue, Oakland
1972 Johnny Bench, Cincinnati	1972 Dick Allen, Chicago
1973 Pete Rose, Cincinnati	1973 Reggie Jackson, Oakland
1974 Steve Garvey, Los Angeles	1974 Jeff Burroughs, Texas
1975 Joe Morgan, Cincinnati	1975 Fred Lynn, Boston
1976 Joe Morgan, Cincinnati	1976 Thurman Munson, New York
1977 George Foster, Cincinnati	1977 Rod Carew, Minnesota
1978 Dave Parker, Pittsburgh	1978 Jim Rice, Boston
1979 (tie) Willie Stargell, Pittsburgh	1979 Don Baylor, California
Keith Hernandez, St. Louis	1980 George Brett, Kansas City
1980 Mike Schmidt, Philadelphia	1981 Rollie Fingers, Milwaukee
1981 Mike Schmidt, Philadelphia	1982 Robin Yount, Milwaukee
1982 Dale Murphy, Atlanta	1983 Cal Ripken Jr., Baltimore
1983 Dale Murphy, Atlanta	1984 Willie Hernandez, Detroit
1984 Ryne Sandberg, Chicago	1985 Don Mattingly, New York
1985 Willie McGee, St. Louis	1986 Roger Clemens, Boston
1986 Mike Schmidt, Philadelphia	1987 George Bell, Toronto
1987 Andre Dawson, Chicago	1988 José Canseco, Oakland
1988 Kirk Gibson, Los Angeles	

USEFUL ADDRESSES

Baseball Commissioner's Office
350 Park Ave.
New York, NY 10022

National League

National League Office
350 Park Ave.
New York, NY 10022

Atlanta Braves
PO Box 4064
Atlanta, GA 30302

Chicago Cubs
Wrigley Field
Chicago, IL 60613

Cincinnati Reds
100 Riverfront Stadium
Cincinnati, OH 45202

Houston Astros
Astrodome
Houston, TX 77001

Los Angeles Dodgers
Dodger Stadium
Los Angeles, CA 90012

Montreal Expos
PO Box 500, Station M
Montreal, Que. H1V 3P2

New York Mets
Shea Stadium
Flushing, NY 11368

Philadelphia Phillies
PO Box 7575
Philadelphia, PA 19101

Pittsburgh Pirates
Three Rivers Stadium
Pittsburgh, PA 15212

St. Louis Cardinals
Busch Stadium
St. Louis, MO 63102

San Diego Padres
PO Box 2000
San Diego, CA 92120

San Francisco Giants
Candlestick Park
San Francisco, CA 94124

American League

American League Office
350 Park Ave.
New York, NY 10022

Baltimore Orioles
Memorial Stadium
Baltimore, MD 21218

Boston Red Sox
24 Yawkey Way
Boston, MA 02215

California Angeles
Anaheim Stadium
Anaheim, CA 92806

Chicago White Sox
324 W. 35th St.
Chciago, IL 60616

Cleveland Indians
Cleveland Stadium
Cleveland, OH 44114

Detroit Tigers
Tiger Stadium
Detroit, MI 48216

Kansas City Royals
Harry S. Truman Sports
Complex
Kansas City, MO 64141

Milwaukee Brewers
Milwaukee County Stadium
Milwaukee, WI 53214

Minnesota Twins
501 Chicago Ave. South
Minneapolis, MN 55415

New York Yankees
Yankee Stadium
Bronx, NY 10451

Oakland A's
Oakland Coliseum
Oakland, CA 94621

Seattle Mariners
100 S. King St.
Seattle, WA 98104

Texas Rangers
1200 Copeland Rd.
Arlington, TX 76011

Toronto Blue Jays
Box 7777
Adelaide St. PO
Toronto, Ont. M5C 2K7

INDEX

PHOTO CREDITS

AP 17, 27, 48, 65, 95, 101, 103, 107, 108 **Baltimore Sun** 26, 41 **Bob Bartosz** 59, 60-61, 68 **Henry Groskinsky** 7, 8, 9, 98 **Steve Hill and Mark Rucker** 48 **Los Angeles Post** 42A **National Baseball Library, Cooperstown, NY** 6, 8, 12A, 13, 14-15, 16, 18, 19, 20, 21, 22, 23, 24, 25, 29, 30, 31, 31B, 33, 35, 36A, 36B, 38A, 39, 40, 42B, 43, 52, 56, 57, 59, 61, 62, 63, 69, 71, 72, 73, 75, 76, 78, 85, 86, 87, 88, 89, 91, 92, 93, 102, 105, 115, 116, 117, 119A, 120 **Rochester Times Union** 45 **San Francisco Bulletin** 49 **St. Louis Post Dispatch** 54-55 **San Diego Union Tribune** 51 **UPI** 58, 67, 83, 104, 110-111, 114 **Wide World** 10, 46-47, 112